WEST AFRICAN
FOLK TALES

HUGH VERNON-JACKSON

ILLUSTRATED BY
PATRICIA WRIGHT

DOVER PUBLICATIONS, INC.
MINEOLA, NEW YORK

Bibliographical Note

This Dover edition, first published in 2003, is an unabridged republication of the text and illustrations from *West African Folk Tales,* Books One and Two (1958), and *More West African Folk Tales,* Books One and Two (1963). Newly reset in one volume, the original four books were compiled by Hugh Vernon-Jackson and first published in London by The University of London Press, Ltd. The separate prefaces from each of the four books have been abridged and combined for the present edition.

Library of Congress Cataloging-in-Publication Data

West African folk tales / [compiled by] Hugh Vernon-Jackson ; illustrated by Patricia Wright.
     p. cm.
    "Unabridged republication of the text and illustrations from West African Folk Tales, Books One and Two (1958), and More West African Folk Tales, Books One and Two (1963)"—T.p. verso.
    Summary: Presents twenty-one traditional tales from West Africa, including "The Greedy but Cunning Tortoise," "The Boy in the Drum," and "The Magic Cooking Pot."
    ISBN 0-486-42764-1 (pbk.)
    1. Tales—Africa, West. 2. Tales—Nigeria. [1. Folklore—Africa, West.] I. Title: West African folktales. II. Vernon-Jackson, Hugh. III. Wright, Patricia, ill. IV. More West African folk tales.

PZ8.1.W4875 2003
398.2'0966—dc21

2002041722

Manufactured in the United States of America
Dover Publications, Inc., 31 East 2nd Street, Mineola, N.Y. 11501

Preface

MANY FOLK TALES from many different parts of the world express similar ideas and sometimes have much the same narrative. Is this yet another example of a universal brotherhood of man, of peoples? African stories are no exception to this; nor are those from Nigeria, which make up this collection.

Some of these stories might in one way or another be familiar to the reader. Part of the pleasure of hearing or reading folk stories is the sense of reminiscence; and also the expectation of what events one feels almost sure are going to happen.

Most of these folk tales were collected from school children in West Africa. They are stories the children themselves liked to tell. The stories are the adventures of men, women, and children as well as those of lions, monkeys, tortoises, and birds. As in many folk tales, there are lessons to be learnt. It appears that wrongdoing does not really succeed, while doing right will triumph in the end.

I am indebted to the many young African men and women who helped in the telling and in the collection of these stories which are from many tribes and many places and are meant to be read for enjoyment.

Although the stories were collected from people of Nigeria's Northern, Eastern, and Western Regions, they should also be of interest in Ghana and other countries, for folk tales are worldwide, and there have been folk tales among all of us ever since the world began.

HUGH VERNON-JACKSON

Contents

The Story of a Hunter and his Antelope Wife

Once upon a time there lived a hunter. He knew much about the ways of animals, but not enough to keep his antelope wife.

One day when he was out hunting in the forest he came to a pool where animals used to come to drink. The hunter hid himself, and while he was watching, a herd of antelope appeared. He prepared his bow and his arrows, but the antelopes did not bend their heads down to drink. Instead, they took off their skins and changed their shapes to become like human beings. They dressed themselves in fine clothes, and the hunter heard them say to each other that they were going to the nearby market.

After they had gone, the hunter went to where they had hung their skins.

"I shall take one of these skins," said the hunter to himself, "and then I shall wait to see these strange antelopes when they come back."

The hunter chose the best skin, and then climbed into a tall tree overlooking the pool.

When evening came and the sun was setting, the creatures returned. They took their skins, put them on over their human forms, and became antelopes again. But one of them, who was in the shape of a young and beautiful woman, could not find her skin.

The other antelopes helped her look for her skin. But it was

nowhere to be found because the hunter had taken it. Finally, the antelopes went on their way, leaving behind the one who could not find her skin.

The antelope woman began to cry, and the hunter, seeing that all the other antelopes had gone, came down from the tree in which he had been hiding.

"Why are you crying, young woman?" the hunter asked.

At first the antelope woman would not tell him.

"You can trust me to keep your secrets," the hunter promised her.

At last the antelope woman admitted that she had lost her skin which would have made her an antelope again.

"I now have no home and do not know what to do," she cried.

"You must marry me," said the hunter, and he told her about his family and that she would be welcome in his compound.

"Your other wife will learn my secrets from you," said the antelope woman.

The hunter assured her that his other wife would never be told about her secrets. Finally, the antelope woman agreed to marry the hunter. He then admitted that it was he who had taken her skin, but she said she would still marry him. Thus she followed him along the paths of the forest back to his compound.

"Where does your new wife come from?" the hunter's first wife asked, but the hunter never told her the truth. Sometimes he said she was the daughter of another hunter; sometimes he said she came from a distant village on the other side of the forest.

The hunter and his new wife lived happily together for some years, and they had three children. However, the hunter's first wife was always curious about the wife who had been brought out from the forest.

"Where is your father's home?" she asked the antelope woman many times.

"Far away," the antelope woman told her, but never said anything more.

One day, the hunter's first wife made some very excellent palm wine from the juices of a palm tree which a man had sold to her. It was such good-tasting palm wine that the hunter drank too much of it. The first wife saw her chance.

"Tell me, husband," she asked, "tell me where your second wife *really* comes from."

The hunter was not in control of his senses. After a little more urging he told all the secrets of his antelope wife.

The next day the two wives quarrelled. They quarrelled about how much rice and soup made of meat should be given to the antelope woman's three children and how much to the first wife's children who were bigger and older. The first wife became very angry.

"Do not be so proud," she cried, "you are only an antelope and your skin is hanging from the roof in our husband's room."

The antelope woman, seeing that her secret had been discovered, decided to return immediately to the forest. Quickly, she went to her husband's room and took down the skin from where it had been hanging. She soaked the skin in a pot of water and measured it to the size of her body; she soaked it and pulled it until it fitted her once again and she changed herself back to the shape of an antelope. Meanwhile, her husband and her three children were away, working on their ground-nut farm.

Running with speed, the antelope woman left the compound and bounded along the path through the high grasses which lead to the ground-nut farm.

When she came to the farm, she beat her three children with her tail, and instantly they changed into handsome young antelopes.

"Farewell!" she cried to her husband, "you have been good to me and to my children, but now your first wife knows my secret."

"Stay, stay," the husband begged.

"We must go for ever!" the antelope woman cried, and with her children she ran down the path and disappeared into the forest.

The husband returned, very angrily, to his compound and drove his first wife away from his house.

The Tortoise and the Leopard

Once upon a time there was a tortoise who lived in a forest. She was a large, fat tortoise with a green and brown shell on her back, and over her stomach she wore a yellow shell.

One day she was going for a walk in the dark, shady forest where she lived. She came to the edge of the forest beside a river, and in the sand beside the river she found some big eggs. She recognized them as being the eggs of a crocodile.

Now the tortoise was very fond of eating good food, and she knew that crocodile eggs have a delicious flavour. She picked up the eggs and hurried with them to the compound of a family which lived near the river.

After the tortoise had greeted the family and the family had greeted the tortoise, she said, "Please, may I enter your compound, for I have something to tell you?"

"Certainly," replied the chief man of the compound, and he and his family allowed the tortoise to enter.

"If you let me use a cooking pot," said the tortoise, "and some firewood, some oil, and some pepper, and if you let me use three big stones to support the cooking pot over the fire, I will make a magic cake for you with the eggs which I am carrying. After you have eaten the magic cake you will always have good luck."

The chief of the compound and his family agreed to what the tortoise suggested. They brought a cooking pot, firewood, oil, pepper, and three big stones to support the cooking pot over the fire. The tortoise asked them to put everything in the room where the family stored its corn. When everything was made ready, the tortoise thanked the family, entered the room and shut and bolted the door.

All day the tortoise cooked the crocodile eggs. She mixed them with the oil and the pepper and the corn which was stored in the room, and she made a very large cake.

When night came and the family were sleeping, the tortoise put the cake in a bag, left the compound very quietly and then ran quickly into the forest.

The next morning the people in the compound woke up. They looked for the tortoise but they could not find her. They knew they had been tricked.

Meanwhile, the tortoise was going deep into the forest carrying the bag with the cake inside it. The day became very dark,

for there were many clouds in the sky. The tortoise heard thunder; then she felt rain. The day became darker and darker, the rain became heavier and heavier. The tortoise was beaten by the rain, but she did not dare return to the compound where she had cooked her cake, so she went on and on, hoping to find shelter. At last she came to the top of a little hill where, through the clearing in the trees, she could see smoke. The tortoise knew that the smoke came from a house and that where there was a house there was shelter. She walked and walked while the rain became stronger and stronger. At last she reached the house.

"Greetings, friend," the tortoise called at the doorway, "please will you let me in, for I am tired and wet from the rain?"

It was a leopard that came to the door.

"Greetings," said the leopard. "Come in."

Inside the house the tortoise found a warm place near the fire. She took her bag with the cake in it, and hung it up on a bamboo pole inside the house. As night had come by that time, the tortoise said good night to the leopard and went to sleep beside the fire.

The next morning when the tortoise woke up she saw that her bag was empty and that the cake had disappeared. It had been eaten by the leopard. The tortoise feared the leopard, so she did not say anything about the cake. Instead, she said, "I thank you, leopard, for giving me shelter. Now, if you will do what I say, I will make a magic powder for you. The magic powder will make you successful whenever you go out hunting."

The foolish leopard was very pleased and he agreed to do what the tortoise said.

The tortoise said that he should go out into the forest and bring forked sticks, four of them, each about six feet high. This the leopard did. The tortoise then said that the leopard should bring two strong poles to be tied on the tops of the forked sticks. The leopard went into the forest again and brought back the poles, tied them to the forked sticks, and drove one end of each forked stick firmly into the ground.

Then he allowed the tortoise to tie him to the poles and sticks.

"When will you untie me?" asked the leopard.

"Never," replied the tortoise. "You ate my cake without asking my permission to eat it. Therefore I shall not untie you. I shall leave you to your fate."

The tortoise then ran off and disappeared in the thick forest.

After several hours some monkeys passed the leopard.

"Monkeys," said the leopard, "please untie me."

"Not us," replied the monkeys, "we are too frightened of you."

The monkeys went on their way. The leopard became very hungry. After several more hours an old mother monkey passed the leopard.

"Oh, Monkey," cried the leopard, "please untie me. I have been here for a long time."

The old mother monkey came back.

"Very well," she said to the leopard, "although I fear you, I will untie you."

The monkey freed the leopard, but she was not free from him. The leopard jumped on her and ate her up. After that, with a roar of rage, he ran into the forest to look for the tortoise.

The leopard went through the forest, but he could not find the tortoise. The leopard went beside the forest near the river, but still he could not find the tortoise. For ever afterwards the leopard searched beside the forest, and whenever one sees a leopard beside a forest, one knows he is looking for a tortoise.

An Elephant, a Bush Dog,
and the Villagers

Once near a village there lived a large and angry elephant, who frightened everyone. The villagers had tried but they had not been able to kill the elephant or drive him away. In fact, they were very often too frightened to leave their houses in case the elephant tried to kill them.

The village head held a meeting in the entrance hall of his compound.

"He who destroys this elephant," he announced, "will be given a large reward worth many pounds."

Encouraged by the thought of a large reward, the best hunters in the village dared to go out and shoot at the elephant with their bows and arrows. All failed.

At last a wild dog from the bush thought he would try for the reward. He went to the village head and said that he would kill the elephant.

"If you are successful," the village head told him, "I will give you good food and a mattress, and let you live in my comfortable house instead of living in the bush. You shall also receive the large reward worth many pounds."

The wild bush dog said that the villagers would have to clear a stretch of ground twenty miles long and a quarter of a mile wide and that it must be straight. The village head arranged for the work to be done when the elephant was not near the village.

When it had been done, the wild bush dog went to the elephant.

"I should like to have a running race with you," the wild bush dog said to him.

"What do you mean by that?" the elephant asked.

"I should like to prove," the wild bush dog replied, "that I am able to run faster than you."

"Nonsense!" said the elephant.

"Prove it!" said the wild bush dog.

The elephant and the wild bush dog then arranged that they would have a race on the following day.

The wild bush dog left the elephant and went to the other wild bush dogs to ask for their help.

"Why should we?" they asked.

"If the elephant is killed, the village people will go farther away from their houses," the wild bush dog replied, "and we shall then be able to catch them and eat them ourselves."

The other wild bush dogs agreed that such words were wise; they said they would give help.

"There are twenty of you here," said the wild bush dog. "One of you will be the starter; you others will each go to a hiding-place in the grass. You will hide beside the running track which the villagers have been foolish enough to clear. Each will hide one mile apart."

The next morning each wild dog was in his position. The leader of the wild bush dogs and the elephant joined the starter at one end of the running track.

The starter cried "Go!" The elephant and the wild bush dog started running. After they had gone one mile the waiting wild bush dog quickly took the place of the other, and the exchange was unnoticed by the elephant. After the next mile another wild bush dog took the place of the other, and so on for every mile, and never once did the elephant notice. At the end of the race the mighty elephant was utterly exhausted and he fell down dead.

"Now," the wild bush dog said, "I shall go and collect my reward." And he told the other bush dogs that they should watch the paths and the farms, because the villagers would be coming out again and could now be caught.

But when the treacherous wild bush dog reached the village,

he found that the village head and all his people had taken advantage of the time when the elephant and the wild bush dogs were racing. They had packed their loads and their food, their goods and all their belongings, and they had fled. They had all run away to a far-distant place.

The Story of a Farmer
and Four Hyenas

Once upon a time there was a farmer named Musa, who lived in a village five miles away from the nearest town. He was very pleased when his wife gave birth to a baby boy.

"It is the custom that you should have very good meals of meat for the next seven days," Musa said to his wife.

"With pepper," his wife replied.

"Pepper and meat I shall buy for you," said Musa, "when I go to the town."

On the following day Musa walked through the forest and the high grass of the bush to the town which was well known for its market. As Musa approached the market he could hear the drums beating which told him that the butchers had fresh meat for sale.

First of all, Musa bought a pocketful of red peppers. Next, he went to the butchers.

"Let me have four legs of a cow," Musa asked the butchers. "My wife has given birth to a baby boy and I must give her much meat that is sweet for her to eat."

"The legs make excellent soup," said the butchers as they gave the meat to Musa, "together with peppers."

Musa paid for the meat, and then spent the rest of the day visiting friends and relatives in the town. In each compound which he entered and to each friend whom he met in the street he said, "My wife has given birth to a boy."

Each friend and each relative replied, "I see that you have much meat to take back to her."

In the evening, after the priest outside the mosque had called

12

for prayers, Musa left the town for his home. On his shoulders he carried the four legs of the cow.

Before he had travelled two miles it became dark. Now the part of the country through which Musa was walking was infested with very fierce hyenas. Soon Musa heard their laughing, and he began to walk quickly. Suddenly, in an open space beside the path, there was a rush of feet and movement on the sandy soil, and Musa was looking into the yellow eyes of a hyena. Musa at first stood still with fright, and then suddenly started to run as fast as he could go. The hyena came quickly after him, preparing to attack. In despair Musa threw down one of the cow-legs which he was carrying. While the hyena stopped to eat the meat, Musa ran on.

Before long, however, Musa heard another hyena laughing. He found another hyena in front of him, on the path. Again, Musa threw a cow-leg to the hyena, and while the hyena stopped to eat the meat, Musa ran on quickly, as quickly as he could go, and faster than he had run before.

But again another hyena appeared and threatened to attack. This hyena was larger and fiercer than the two others had been. Again, Musa threw a cow-leg to the hyena, and while the hyena stopped to eat the meat, Musa ran on as quickly as he could go.

Now Musa remembered that there was a small village not far from where he was and nearer than his own village. He turned and followed a narrow path which led to the nearer village, all the time running very fast.

But for the fourth time a hyena suddenly appeared. This hyena was even larger than the one before had been.

"I will eat you," growled the hyena and jumped towards Musa. Without hesitation Musa threw the last cow-leg to the hyena, knowing that there was nothing left to throw for hyenas to eat except himself.

He ran on and on until to his relief he saw in the distance the glimmering of a light which told him that he had nearly reached the village.

As he was running towards the light, he found that all four hyenas were now chasing him. He tried to call for help, but he was so breathless that he had lost his voice. Just before the hyenas were near enough to catch him, he managed to reach the village and entered the first house he came to, where there were many people inside the entrance hall, sitting round a brightly burning fire. Musa fell on the floor, unable at first to talk, and breathing hard because he had been running so fast for so long.

The laughing of the hyenas outside the house told the villagers that Musa had been chased. The villagers seized their knives and axes and ran out to frighten the animals away. When they returned, they gave Musa some food and a place to sleep.

The next morning Musa thanked his protectors and returned to his own village. He told his wife what had happened and how he had lost the cow-legs.

"Only the pocket of peppers have I brought you," he said.

"Better that you lose everything," his good wife replied, "as long as you return safely yourself to your wife and child."

The next day Musa went back to the market in the town. He had only enough money left to buy one cow-leg. He told everyone his misfortune and his adventure, and there was no one who did not help him. The money he was given was enough to buy three more cow-legs.

The drums were beating and the butchers were again selling meat. Musa bought four cow-legs once more, thanking his good fortune. Not waiting for the night, but in the sunshine of the afternoon he hurried back to his village. On the way he thought he heard hyenas in the grass, but he was not sure; he thought he saw yellow eyes, but he was not sure. But he reached home safely. Thick soup was made for his wife. She grew strong. The baby boy grew well, and Musa and his family lived happily ever after.

The Greedy but Cunning Tortoise

O nce upon a time there lived on a hill an old and selfish tortoise. He was also a cunning tortoise.

This old, selfish, and cunning tortoise had a wife who knew how to cook delicious food and how to make very good soup.

The tortoise and his wife had a large compound. In it they kept dogs, cats, goats, hens, and ducks. Some belonged to the tortoise, and some belonged to his wife.

Now as well as being old, selfish, and cunning, the tortoise was also greedy. One by one he killed and ate all his share of the dogs, cats, goats, hens, and ducks. His wife cooked this food for him but he gave her very little of it to eat, for he wanted to eat as much as he could by himself. The tortoise's wife did not mind. "It is the way of my husband's character," she thought, "and I am used to it."

After the tortoise had eaten his share, he said that he would like to start eating the dogs, cats, goats, hens, and ducks which belonged to his wife.

"No," said his wife. "I will not let you eat my animals." She would not listen to his begging. "Nor will I let you eat my hens and my ducks," she said.

The tortoise planned to deceive his wife and by trickery to obtain what he wanted. He pretended to be very ill.

"Go quickly and pray," the tortoise told his wife, "and ask how I can be cured."

As soon as his wife had gone into the woods to pray, the tortoise left the mat on which he had been lying, and by another path went to the place where he knew his wife would pray. He

15

hid himself in a hole and waited for his wife to come. When she arrived, the tortoise heard her ask how she could cure her husband's illness.

"No one can help your husband," the tortoise replied from his hole, speaking in a strange, deep voice, "but you yourself."

His wife prayed again, asking how she could help him.

"Unless you give your husband your fattest goats and fattest animals, and also your fattest hens and ducks," the tortoise answered, "your husband is sure to die."

The wife was very grateful for an answer to her prayer and she hurried off on her way home.

As soon as she had gone the tortoise crawled out of the hole and ran as fast as he could by a short path and reached his house before his wife returned. There he lay down again on his mat and pretended still to be sick.

When his wife came back, she told the tortoise what she would do to help him.

"It is good news," said the tortoise. "Now bring me your fattest goats and fattest animals, and also your fattest hens and ducks."

When the wife brought her fattest animals and birds, the tortoise took them off into the woods. He told his wife not to follow, and he walked slowly like a sick man until he was out of sight of his wife. Then he ran very fast.

When the tortoise reached a small farm which he had in the middle of the woods, he killed all the fat animals as well as the fat hens and fat ducks. He cut them into small pieces and put them into a large black pot which he kept at his farm. He built a fire between three large stones and then put the pot of meat on top.

As the meat was cooking, the smell became very sweet. The tortoise thought, "I shall enjoy eating this meat very much."

The tortoise then went away from the fire to look for crickets in their holes, because he wanted to eat crickets together with all his meat. While he was looking for the crickets a large and ugly creature all covered with long hair crawled out of one of the cricket holes.

"I smell your food cooking," said the ugly creature. "Carry me to where your food is cooking, tortoise."

The tortoise refused.

"Greedy tortoise," the creature cried angrily and said some magic words. At once, the tortoise's mouth and nose began to close. "Unless you do what I say," said the creature, "your mouth and nose will never open again."

The tortoise led the creature to where his meat was cooking. His mouth and nose opened, but not until the creature had eaten all the meat, every piece of it, and the tortoise was left with nothing.

"Now take me to your house," the creature said.

The tortoise took the ugly, hairy creature back to his house, and all the people were frightened of it. It lay down in the tortoise's room and went to sleep. While the creature slept the tortoise and his wife set fire to the room and burnt it down.

When the fire had burnt itself out, the tortoise looked inside the room. There were blackened ruins. The creature was inside, well roasted and smelling like very good-tasting food.

"I shall eat the roasted creature," the greedy tortoise said.

His wife advised him not to, but he ignored her.

When he had finished eating the creature, the head of the tortoise began to grow larger and larger. If the walls of his burnt room had not crumbled, the tortoise would not have been able to get out because his head became larger than the little doorway.

Now the cunning tortoise planned a way by which he could exchange his big head for a small one. He saw a ram on his way to the river to take a bath. At that time rams had very small heads. The tortoise followed the ram.

"I too shall have a bath in the river," said the tortoise to the ram.

"Very well," the ram replied.

In those days it was the custom for animals to take off their heads and leave them on the river-bank before entering the water. The ram and the tortoise took off their heads. While the ram was bathing the tortoise quietly climbed out of the river; he fitted the ram's small head to his neck and very quickly ran away.

When the tortoise reached home, he and his wife put their belongings in baskets and ran away from the hill on which they lived. They went to a faraway valley.

"We shall build our new house here," said the tortoise, and they did.

Meanwhile, the ram had finished his bath, but on leaving the river found that his head had been taken away. Angry as he was, he had to have a head, so he put on the big one which the tortoise had left.

The ram ran to where the tortoise had once lived.

"Where is that cunning tortoise?" the ram cried, but no one knew where the tortoise and his wife had gone.

Promising himself that one day he would find and punish the tortoise, the ram went away. But he never found the tortoise and he had to keep his big head. That is why the ram's head is big and the tortoise's head is small: it is an exchange of heads.

The One-legged Man and the Tortoise

There was a tortoise who lived near a certain village where the people were very prosperous, but he was not very well off himself. The tortoise planned how he would steal food from the prosperous villagers.

First, he killed a giant rat, and used its skin for making a drum and the bones for making flutes.

When the tortoise had finished making his drum and his flutes, he called his friends from the village to come for a feast. They came at night when the moon was high and round. When they had arrived, the tortoise gave them food, and then gathering them in the courtyard of his compound he started to play his drum. Whilst he himself played his drum, his children played the flutes. At the sound of the drum and flutes the villagers began to dance, for they could not help themselves. They danced until they were exhausted, and even then they danced until they lost their senses. As the dawn was breaking, the tortoise told the villagers to go home, and as they left they thanked the tortoise for his kindness.

After two weeks, the tortoise found that he and his family had no more food to eat.

"Now is the time," the tortoise said to his wife, "to prove the trick which I have planned."

The tortoise and his wife took the drum and the flutes and went to the prosperous village where there was plenty of food. They hid among high grasses and bushes not far from the village well, but where the people could not see them. When evening

19

came, the tortoise started to make music with his drum and there was also the sound of flutes.

When the people heard the drumming they left their work. They left whatever they were doing. They left their food and started to dance. While they were dancing the tortoise told his wife and family to go into the empty houses and take away as much food as they could. Then the tortoise and his family hurried away in the darkness.

After the drumming and dancing was over, the village people found that much of their food had gone, and so they were hungry.

Again and again the tortoise would come to the village at evening time and play his music. Again and again the people could not resist the sound of the drumming and they left everything in order to dance. Each time the tortoise and his family would steal what food the villagers had collected.

The people went to their king, and told him what was happening to them, complaining that they were losing their food.

"Please give us help to find out the trouble and rid us of it," the people begged, "otherwise we shall all have to run away and leave your village."

The king called to his palace all his councillors and the important men of the village and they discussed ways in which they might find out who was doing the drumming. They chose a powerful wizard to find out for them, but the next night, when the drumming started and the wizard went towards the sound to find out who was responsible, he too was caught by the music and started to dance. Meanwhile, the tortoise's family were carrying away the food of the village.

The king again called to his palace all his councillors and the important men of the village. He also called everyone else in the village to come.

"I will give one hundred pounds," the king declared, "to the man who finds out who is drumming and stealing our food."

After he had spoken those words, a one-legged man, leaning on a piece of stick, came slowly forward until he was in front of the king.

"May your life be long," the one-legged man said to the king. "I will find out who is drumming and stealing the food."

At the sight of the one-legged man offering to try for the reward, many people laughed and many said he was foolish. But the one-legged man again asked for permission to try, and the king agreed.

"I wish you success in trying to find out who is drumming and stealing our food," said the king. "I order you to try."

On that same night the tortoise came again to the village. Again he played his drum, and while the people danced his family began stealing the food. Only the one-legged man did not dance. He heard the music and he wanted to dance, but with only one leg he could not. Therefore he went into the tall grass, where he saw the tortoise drumming. After this he went into the houses, where he saw the family of the tortoise carrying away the food.

The next day the one-legged man went to the palace to see the king.

"May your life be long," he said to the king. "I have found out who is drumming and stealing your food."

"Speak," ordered the king. "Tell us who is causing us this great trouble."

"The tortoise," said the one-legged man.

When they heard the news, the villagers were filled with wonder at the trick which the tortoise had played on them. They rushed, all of them, to the tortoise's house and drove him and his family away. They drove them so far away that the tortoise could never return.

"My villagers and I are grateful for your help," said the king to the one-legged man.

The king gave the man the hundred pounds which had been promised as a reward. The man was overjoyed. He built himself a house and a compound in that village and he sent for his family to live with him. He had many sons and they made many farms. He became a councillor to the king and he gave wisdom to the village for the rest of his long life.

A She-goat and her Children

Once upon a time a she-goat told her children that they would go out into the world to seek their fortune.

They set out and reached a cave when night came. When they entered the cave in order to find shelter for the night, they met a hyena inside.

"Welcome to you," said the hyena. "I will give you food and water."

The she-goat thanked the hyena.

"I will go to fetch water for you," said the hyena.

The she-goat thanked the hyena again, but said that she and her children had decided not to drink.

"I will grind corn for you," said the hyena. The she-goat thanked the hyena, but said she would grind it herself.

The she-goat started to grind corn on a stone and as she worked she sang a song.

"My teeth are blunt," she sang, "and my mouth is tired, because I have been eating elephant and lion today.

Hyena, I come to you.

What would you have me do to you?"

When the hyena heard this song, she ran out of the cave and into the bush. Then the she-goat said to her children, "If I had not played this trick, the hyena would have killed us."

After eating their meal, the she-goat and her children lay down on the floor of the cave and went to sleep.

The next morning they got up and travelled all day along the road until night came. Again they found a cave and entered it in

order to shelter for the night. But inside the cave there was a lioness.

When the lioness saw the she-goat and her children, she roared; she roared because she thought she would kill the she-goat and her children.

Then the she-goat started to sing.

"My teeth are blunt," she sang, "and my mouth is tired, because I have been eating elephant and lion today.

Lioness, I come to you.

What would you have me do to you?"

The children of the she-goat also started to sing.

"To be able to fight," they sang,

"To fight is our great delight.

We made the hyena run from us yesterday."

When the lioness heard this, she ran out of the cave and into the bush. Then the she-goat and her children ate the food of the lioness.

"We should thank ourselves," said the she-goat, "for playing this trick. Otherwise the lioness would have killed us."

They lay down on the floor of the cave and went to sleep.

The next morning they got up and travelled all day along the road until night came, when they reached a certain town where all the women were wicked. They entered the compound of the oldest, most wicked woman in the town.

"Welcome," said the wicked old woman, "and spend the night in my house. I will give you food to eat and water to drink."

The she-goat and her children thanked the wicked old woman and entered her compound.

"Here is guinea corn and here is a grinding stone," said the wicked old woman. "You must grind the corn so that you will have food to eat."

Then the she-goat started to sing.

"My teeth are blunt," she sang, "and my mouth is tired, because I have been eating elephant and lion today.

Wicked old woman, I come to you.

What would you have me do to you?"

The children of the she-goat also started to sing.

"To be able to fight,

To fight is our great delight.
We made the lioness run from us yesterday."

When the wicked old woman heard this she went everywhere in the town saying that the she-goat and her children had eaten elephant and lion and had made the lioness run away. Then the wicked old woman and all the people heard the she-goat and her children sing another song:

"Run away, run away," they sang.
"It is men and wicked women,
We shall eat today."

The people of the town became very frightened. Then, seizing their belongings, they left the town and scattered. They left the town to the she-goat and her children.

The she-goat said to her children, "If we had not played this trick, the wicked old woman would have killed us; she would have eaten our meat and made our skins into mats for the floor of her compound."

Then the she-goat and her children went to live in the deserted town, and ate the food that was there. They made their homes there, because they had succeeded in their cleverness.

How the Hyena's Fur became Striped

Once upon a time there lived a spider, whose neighbour was a hyena.

One day the spider and the hyena decided to go together to the river. When they reached the banks of the wide river they met the king of the river.

"Long may you live," said the spider and the hyena to the king of the river, saluting him.

"Greetings to you," said the king of the river, and as a present he gave them many fish.

After the king of the river had left them, the spider and the hyena made a fire. The spider sat beside the fire cooking the fish and as each fish was cooked he threw it over his back so that it should lie on the bank and grow cool. But each time the spider threw a cooked fish over his back the hyena caught it and ate it.

When the spider had finished cooking the fish he turned around to begin eating them. He saw that there were no fish left and he knew that his neighbour had eaten all of them. Tears of anger came into the eyes of the spider.

"Why do you weep?" the hyena asked. "Is it because I have eaten all the fish?"

"No," replied the spider; "you know that when one sits near the fire one's eyes become tired and there are tears."

At that moment a parrot flew past the spider and the hyena, a bird with feathers of many beautiful and bright colours.

The spider thought to himself, "Now I shall have revenge upon the hyena."

He said to the hyena, "Did you see that parrot with the feathers of many beautiful and bright colours?"

The hyena said he had seen the parrot and had admired its plumage.

"It is I," said the spider, "who gave the bird her colours."

"Please, spider," the hyena begged, "will you colour my fur in the same way?"

The spider agreed to colour the fur of the hyena.

"What shall I pay you?" asked the simple hyena.

"Pay me nothing," the cunning spider replied. "Only do whatever I tell you to do."

The spider listened to the words of the grateful hyena, and then told him to go and get a very long rope of strong leather.

When the hyena returned, he brought with him a very long rope of strong leather. The spider told him to lie down beside a tree and tied him tightly to it. The spider then took a piece of wire and put it in the fire on which the fish had been cooked. When the wire was red-hot, he took it to the hyena and burnt him with it.

As the spider burnt the hyena, the spider said, "Now you have your reward for eating all the fish."

When the spider had finished burning the fur of the hyena, he went away, leaving the hyena tied to the tree.

A family of white ants saw the leather rope which bound the hyena. They went to the leather and ate it, freeing the hyena.

"Thank you," said the hyena; "now I ask you to eat the leather which binds my foot."

When they did this, the hyena quickly put the white ants into his mouth and swallowed them. They gave him enough strength to return, very slowly, to his house.

For a long time the hyena lay sick in his house. While he lay there a jackal came to him and helped him. Finally the hyena gained his strength, and getting up from his mat went to the door of his house.

"You are now strong and in good health again," the jackal said to the hyena.

"That is true," the hyena replied, "but my fur is still marked in stripes where the cunning spider burnt me with a hot wire."

That is the reason why hyenas were given stripes, and from that day on all hyenas have had stripes on their fur.

The Boy in the Drum

Long ago there was a man called Yusufu who had a wife named Lade. They had only one son and his name was Hanafi. Because he was their only son, Hanafi was very much loved by his father and mother. His parents, in fact, always gave him everything he wanted and allowed him to do anything he pleased.

As Hanafi grew older he became very fond of hunting. One evening he told his parents that he planned to go hunting that night.

"Please do not go tonight," his mother Lade said. "I feel that tonight is unlucky."

"It is very dangerous," said his father Yusufu. "You are our only son, and we do not want you to risk death in the forest at night."

Hanafi refused to pay any attention to what his father and mother said. Finally they allowed him to go.

Hanafi went into the forest with several friends. They took bows and arrows, knives and guns and also lamps. When the animals came to the light the hunters killed two deer and six hares, and Hanafi was given his share of the meat.

As the hunters started back to their village, there was thunder and lightning in the sky. There was a great wind, and then there was heavy rain.

Hanafi saw a tortoise sitting in its house.

"Please may I have shelter from the rain?" Hanafi asked the tortoise.

"You may indeed have shelter," the cunning tortoise replied. "Here is a big pot you may sit in."

It was dry in the pot, so he thanked the tortoise and crawled inside.

As soon as Hanafi had entered the pot the tortoise took a large piece of skin and covered the mouth of the pot with it. With the skin tied on top the tortoise made the pot into a drum.

The next day the tortoise went to the king of the village.

"Your Majesty," the tortoise begged as he knelt on the floor in front of where the king was sitting, "may we have a drumming competition?"

"A drumming competition is a good idea," said the king. "We shall see who in the village makes his drum sound the best."

Three days later everyone in the village assembled at the palace, and all the skilled drummers also came. With them they brought their drums.

Yusufu, the father of the boy in the tortoise's drum, was amongst the crowd which came to the palace. As the tortoise beat the drum, Hanafi, the boy inside, began to sing. Yusufu heard the voice; he heard the boy singing his own and his father's names.

After the drumming was over, the king praised the tortoise, saying that the sound of his drumming was better than anyone else's. Then Yusufu went to the tortoise.

"Come to my house, tortoise, chief of all drummers," he said, "and you will be given an excellent dinner."

The tortoise thanked Yusufu and followed him to his house at the edge of the village.

While much good food and drink was being given to the tortoise, Yusufu told his wife to boil water. After his meal the tortoise lay down on a mat and went to sleep.

"Quick!" whispered Yusufu to his wife, "we will make him into soup," and they put the tortoise in the boiling water.

"Quick!" cried Yusufu to his wife, "we must save our son Hanafi."

He cut the skin on the tortoise's drum and brought out his son in time to save his life.

Ever after, Hanafi was an obedient boy who lived happily because he followed the advice of his father and mother.

Adamu's Mountain

Once upon a time there was a very large hyena who lived on a mountain. The hyena's dwelling-place was a cave in the mountain-side, and it was so big that a man could stand upright in it.

At the foot of the mountain was a village of farmers and their families. All the people of the village feared the large hyena, and it was their custom to bring many presents to the cave and to treat the hyena with great respect.

One day a man called Adamu came from another village. He asked the people why they took presents to the mountain, but they would not tell him.

"I shall go to see for myself," said Adamu.

Adamu went to the mountain. Climbing the mountain-side, he found the cave and entered it. He walked far inside. Suddenly he looked back and saw the very large hyena.

"Let me out!" cried Adamu, but there was no way out. The hyena stood between Adamu and the door of the cave.

"Why have you entered my house?" the hyena asked in an angry voice.

Adamu could make no reply. He was too frightened.

"You are my prisoner," said the hyena, and he put Adamu in the food store at the back of the cave.

"Later I shall eat you," said the hyena, locking the door.

Meanwhile, Adamu's family, who had been travelling with him, wondered where Adamu could be. But his brother had heard him planning to go up the mountain. After two days the brother went to the chief of the village.

"Let me go to the mountain and look for my brother," he asked the chief.

"We shall look for him," the chief replied, "but we must take a present."

The brother gave the chief one of Adamu's fat goats. The chief, the brother, and many people went up the mountain-side until they reached the cave. The chief took the goat to the cave, and calling in a loud voice begged the hyena to let Adamu come out. Suddenly, Adamu came out.

No one ever saw the hyena again. When the people went back to take presents, the cave had disappeared from the side of the mountain. Ever afterwards it was called "Adamu's Mountain."

The Man with Seven Dogs

There once lived a man called Manma who was a hunter and also a magician.

Manma had seven dogs. Their names were Tabantagi, Guye, Tako, Tifi, Etsuegu, Tazata, and Eyeshisoko. The dogs were well trained and were useful for Manma's hunting. Manma also had seven large black earthenware pots which he kept in his room. The pots helped him in his magic; they helped protect him from his enemies.

As well as the seven dogs and the seven pots, Manma had a wife. Manma and his wife very much wanted to have a child, but to their sorrow they had no children. The only help which Manma could obtain from his magic pots was their advice to ask someone else what he should do, so Manma went to a friend of his who was also a magician, and asked for his advice.

"Unless you have a lion's skin spread in front of your wife," the friend said, "not only will your wife have no child but she will also die."

Manma wasted no time. Taking his gun, he went into the forest, where he soon found a small lion, a cub, which had been left unprotected. Manma blessed his good fortune in finding a lion so quickly. He shot the lion and took the skin to his wife's room. Manma spread the skin in front of his wife and it was not long before she bore a child.

"We have been lucky," Manma said to his wife. "The magic pots directed me to the right man for advice."

Manma went to his seven black pots and told them that they had been successful.

Meanwhile, the lioness in the forest had discovered that her cub was missing. She heard from some monkeys in a tree that Manma had shot it and taken its skin, and she became very angry. The lioness changed herself into a beautiful princess and dressed herself in rich clothes fit for a princess. She then followed the footsteps of Manma which led her to Manma's village.

When the lioness came near the village she met an old woman selling baskets.

"I wish to buy a basket," the lioness said.

"Sixpence," said the old woman.

"I will give you fourpence," the lioness replied. The old woman agreed and the lioness bought the basket.

When she reached the village she went to the market-place where there were many people, and amongst them she saw Manma. Many people greeted the lioness, she having changed herself into the form of a beautiful princess. Many asked her to come and be a guest in their compounds.

"I shall stay," she replied, "in the compound of the man who can throw a stone into my basket."

Many people threw stones, but all missed. Manma was watching, and his companions urged him to try to throw a stone into the basket. Manma threw a stone, and in that first try it fell right into the middle of the basket.

"I shall be your guest," said the lioness who looked like a princess, and she followed him to his compound. The first thing which she saw in his house was the skin of her lion cub.

Manma's wife fed the lioness, and when night came and it was dark the lioness was given a room in which to sleep. In the middle of the night she got up in order to go and kill Manma, but Tabantagi, one of Manma's seven dogs, stopped her.

"We have been warned," Tabantagi said to the lioness, for the seven black pots had spoken to the seven dogs. "If you kill our master, we will eat you."

The lioness went back into her room. After she had waited for a long time, she got up again, in order to go and kill Manma. Guye, however, another of Manma's seven dogs, stopped her.

"If you kill our master we will eat you," Guye said to the lioness.

Again the lioness went back in to her room. Again, after waiting for a long time, she tried to go out to kill Manma. Again, one of the seven dogs stopped her. She tried seven times and seven times she was stopped by the dogs. By that time the night had passed and it was morning.

The lioness saw no way of killing Manma on that visit.

Remaining in the appearance of a princess, the lioness thanked Manma for having her in his house as a guest, and she told him that she would be going away.

"I will escort you out of the village," said Manma, and he took up a gun.

"Are you going to shoot me?" the lioness asked.

Manma put down the gun and took up his bow and arrows.

"Are you going to kill me?" the lioness asked.

Manma put down his bow and arrows and took up a whistle.

"Let us go," he said, and the lioness agreed that they should go.

After Manma had escorted her for over five miles through fields and high grasses, they reached a river. Manma and the lioness said good-bye to each other and Manma began to walk back to his village. After Manma had walked for some distance, he found a locust-bean tree growing beside the path. He managed to climb up the tree just before the lioness, who had changed herself from the shape of a princess into her true shape, sprang at him in order to kill him. She had been following him.

Manma blew very loudly on his whistle. Immediately Manma's seven dogs appeared from the bush grass, first Tabantagi, then Guye, then Tako, followed by Tifi, Etsuegu, Tazata, and Eyeshisoko.

Before the lioness was able to run away, the dogs jumped on her and killed her. The dogs kept the meat and Manma took the skin.

"My wife," said Manma when he reached his house, "we had one child for our one lion skin. Now here is another skin."

The Story of Muhammadu

In olden times there lived a man called Muhammadu, a wood-cutter. The bundles of wood which he collected he brought to the market-place in the town to sell. Unfortunately, where he lived there were not many trees or bushes, so that the work did not bring him much profit.

Muhammadu had no wife, but he worked very hard in order to save enough money to be able to afford one. He dug a hole in the ground in his compound, and in the hole he hid his money. He put in the hole all the money he earned from his wood-cutting, keeping out only what he needed to buy food.

When Muhammadu had collected by his hard work and saved enough money to afford a wife, he dug up his money and left his town. He left behind him the gates and the walls and went to a small village in the bush. In the village he met a girl who agreed to be his wife. Muhammadu therefore went to the father of the girl and the marriage was arranged.

Everyone in the village came to the marriage celebration. There was a great feast, at which Muhammadu's wife received many presents—cloth, basins, pots, and corn. Muhammadu himself bought much corn and many mats, and he bought donkeys to carry the loads.

When it was time for Muhammadu to return to his town, he loaded his donkeys with the cloth, the basins, the mats, the pots, the corn, and all the belongings of himself and his newly married wife. He said farewell to the people in the village and he and his wife set out on their journey.

When they reached the gates and walls of the town,

Muhammadu said to his wife, "This is the town where I live, and here is where we shall settle and prosper. This gate is where we shall enter."

There were many camels and donkeys and people entering the gates. Many of the people were greatly surprised to see Muhammadu the wood-cutter arriving with a wife and with donkeys heavily laden with goods and foodstuffs.

Muhammadu met one of the most important councillors of the town, a man whose title was Galadima. Muhammadu made polite greetings to the Galadima, and then went on with his wife and his possessions to his compound.

During the night thieves entered Muhammadu's compound and bound Muhammadu and his wife with ropes. The thieves had sharp knives, and they said they would kill Muhammadu and his wife if they cried out. So saying, they took the donkeys and the corn, the cloth and everything that was in the compound. They did not leave one pot, they did not leave even a needle.

The next morning Muhammadu and his wife were able to free themselves from the ropes with which the thieves had tied them. When they went out into the street, they told their neighbours what had happened. They went to the great compound of the Galadima in order to tell him their sad story.

Entering the compound of the Galadima, Muhammadu and his wife heard angry voices disputing the division of donkeys, corn, cloth, pots, mats, and other goods. It was the Galadima quarrelling about his share with several men whom Muhammadu recognized as the thieves who had robbed him. Muhammadu cried out to all the people. Pointing to his belongings, he called for justice against the thieves and the Galadima, who was their master.

"They bound us; they threatened to kill us!" Muhammadu cried. "They stole all that I had, I who as a wood-cutter had worked hard and saved my money."

These happenings were quickly carried to the ears of the Emir, who was the king of the town and of all the surrounding country. The Emir took speedy action. He drove the Galadima from the town for ever, he drove away the Galadima's followers and all the people in the Galadima's great compound.

The Emir called Muhammadu the wood-cutter, and the turban of honour was wound around the head of Muhammadu.

The Emir said to Muhammadu, "Now you are the Galadima of my town. You are the Galadima in my council."

For Muhammadu from that day on there was increasing wealth and power.

A Hunter, when the World began

A very long time ago, in the beginning of the world, there lived a famous hunter. He had killed so many wild animals that he had been given the title, King of All Hunters.

The King of All Hunters had two sons. When one of the sons wished to marry a young girl in the town, the King of All Hunters decided to test the strength and cleverness of this son.

"All the wildest, most savage animals I have killed," he said to his son, "except one. Go out into the bush. If you are able to kill this one remaining savage creature you will have permission to marry the young girl."

The young man prepared to go into the bush to hunt the savage creature.

"Remember," his father warned him, "what you are going to hunt is the most fearful animal in the world: with many mouths; with fire-like eyes; with enormous strength."

The young man took some food, then took his gun and his knife, called for his three dogs, and went off into the bush. He walked all day, and in the evening caught a hare for his supper. He walked all the next day and the day after that.

At last he came to the hut of an old woman who lived alone. She was outside her hut by a stream, where she was washing cooking-pots. She called out to him.

"I cannot stop," the young man replied, "for my business is urgent."

The old woman called to him again that it was very important for him to speak with her. The young man turned and went to see what she wanted.

"Here is food," said the old woman.

It was good food and the young man enjoyed eating it.

"Here is a calabash," said the old woman, "please wash it."

The young man went to the stream and started to wash the calabash. But as he washed it, it broke. Inside he found an egg, a round smooth stone, and a small broom of palm-raffia.

"You have broken the calabash and I am glad," said the old woman. "Take with you what you have found inside. In case of danger drop one at a time, first the egg, then the small broom, then the round smooth stone."

The young man thanked her and went on his way.

The next day the young man reached a dark forest. He entered the forest, and at once his dogs started to bark. To his surprise, the young man suddenly saw the fearful creature which he had set out to hunt. The creature had many mouths, and fire-like eyes, and enormous strength.

The young man aimed his gun and fired, but the fearful creature only looked at him and grew bigger and bigger. The young man made a sign to his dogs to attack the fearful creature, but having looked into the fire-like eyes, their own eyes were blinded. The young man took his knife and ran to attack the fearful creature. They fought all that day, all that night, and all the next day, but at last the young man was victorious and killed the fearful creature.

The young man was glad, for he was now certain to marry the young girl in his town, and also he had destroyed a more fearful creature than any other hunter had done. The young man put the fearful creature on his back and started on his homeward journey. He left the forest and was walking through some woods when it became dark. He lay down to sleep.

The next morning was bright and clear, but as the young man woke up he saw coming towards him another animal, far larger than the fearful creature he had killed, far fiercer, and with far more fiery eyes.

The young man jumped up and started to run, with the wild animal following him. He remembered what the old woman had given him, and he dropped the egg. At once, there was a wide lake behind him, the greatest lake in the world. The wild animal still followed him. He dropped the broom, and at once there was the largest forest in the world behind him. The wild animal still followed. But the young man was nearing his father's house. He dropped the round smooth stone, and at once there stood the highest mountain in the world. But the wild animal still followed.

At last the young man reached his father's house.

"Quick, quick!" he cried to his brother who had been left at home, "open the door for me!"

As the young man ran in and the door was closing after him, the wild animal reached out and seized what he could from the young man's back before the young man escaped. And that is how the young man lost his tail and why no man in the world after that ever had a tail.

The Son with a Big Head

There was once a small boy whose parents lived in a small town on the top of a steep hill. The boy's mother and sister had to work very hard every day going down the hill to the well, drawing the water from the well, putting the water in earthenware jars on their shoulders and carrying it up the hill.

As he grew, the small boy's head grew bigger and bigger, until it was almost as big as the hill on which his parents lived. The boy not only had a huge head, but he also drank a great quantity of water all the time and he refused to eat food.

Finally, the parents went down the hill in despair to ask the advice of an old man who made medicines.

"Here is some medicine," said the old man to the parents. "Make your big-headed son take the medicine three times a day. Then see what happens to this over-thirsty boy."

When the parents went up the hill again they gave their son the medicine, three times a day. When he had taken the medicine for a few days, the big-headed boy stopped asking for so much water and began to eat food.

His parents were very pleased to see him eating, but the next day the boy ate all the food that could be found in his parents' own house. He continued to eat a great quantity of food every day for three weeks, and after this there was no food left in his family's compound. Then he ate all the food in the town. When the people of the town saw that they were left without food, they went to the king of the town with their complaint. They told the king what the big-headed boy had done.

"Bring the big-headed boy to me!" ordered the king.

But when the people went to the compound where the boy lived, they could not find him.

"If you find the big-headed boy, kill him," ordered the king.

But the people still could not find the big-headed boy, so they went back to the king and told him.

The king then called his councillors to his palace, and all the people were also called. They discussed what they should do. They decided not to kill the big-headed boy; instead, they would all leave the town while he was sleeping.

The next day, while the big-headed boy was sleeping during the heat of early afternoon, all the people quietly left the town. After they had gone down the hill and travelled several miles, the boy's sister stopped.

"I have forgotten my spoon," she said. "I left it in our house on top of the hill."

Her parents said they would buy her a new spoon when they reached the next town.

"No," said the sister. "I must go back for my own spoon."

She refused to go on, saying that she had to go back to fetch her spoon, and she went back up the hill.

When she reached the house, she found that the big-headed boy had woken up.

"Where have all the people gone?" he asked.

"They have run away," his sister answered. "You have been eating all their food."

"We must go after them together," said the big-headed boy.

"You can't come with me," she replied.

"Why don't you want me to go with you?" he asked.

"If you go with me," said the sister, "everyone will beat me, and you will eat all their food."

However, the sister had to go back, and the big-headed boy followed her. On their way the sister asked him whether he had any idea as to how they might have a meal, for they were both tired and hungry and it was clear that all the people had gone on without waiting.

"You will soon have a meal," the big-headed boy replied.

He began to chant many extraordinary words, as in a song,

and after a few minutes a crowd of people appeared carrying animals, clothes, and food.

The big-headed boy asked the people to build houses of good shapes and with strong walls. This they did, building them very quickly beside a river of clear water. The people then settled in the houses they had built, and the big-headed boy with his sister settled with them. Every day the people supplied the big-headed boy with all the food he needed. Every day the boy's body became larger and stronger, and his head became smaller, until at last he was a handsome man.

The people gathered together, and agreed that the big-headed boy who had so quickly changed should be their king.

"Will you be our king?" the people asked.

"Yes," the man replied, "from today I will be your king."

A fine, large house with many rooms and courtyards was built for him, and this was his palace. The new king ordered that the people build another fine house for his faithful sister.

One day, when the king was sitting in the great hall of his palace, an old old man came in to see him.

"I know who you are," said the old old man.

"Where have you seen me before?" the king asked.

"Were you not the boy whose parents ran away together with all the people of a town because you ate all their food and had a very big head?"

"I was," the king replied, "and now I am a king."

The king asked the old old man where he lived.

"I live in the town," he replied, "where your mother and father now live. I am going back there now, and I hope you will go with me in order to see your parents."

The king put on his expensive clothes, and he followed the old old man to the town where his parents lived. It was not far away, and they soon reached the house of the parents.

When the parents saw their son, handsome and in his expensive clothes, followed by servants, they made humble greetings and salutations.

"Long may you live, Your Highness!" they said.

"My greetings to you," said the king. "Do you not know me?"

"We do not know you," his parents answered.

The king returned to his town and to his palace, and asked his wife to cook bowlfuls of excellent food to be sent to his parents. He asked his servants to take the food to his parents but not to allow them to eat it, for they were to uncover the bowls and the servants were to bring back the food after his parents had seen it.

When the servants reached the parents' house they did what they had been asked to do. They uncovered the bowls of food and showed it to the parents but refused to let them eat. Then the servants returned to the palace with the food. The parents followed them, and entered the palace. In the palace the servants gave the food to the king, but the parents still did not know that the king was their son.

"Why have you followed my servants?" the king asked them.

"Because we have no food of our own and we are hungry," the parents answered. "We want to eat the food which they showed us."

Then the king told them that he was their son whom they had left in the town on the hill to die without food. When the parents heard this they wept and they wailed and they cried.

The heart of the king softened, and he ordered his servants to bring more and better food for his parents.

"You are my father and mother, so you shall eat," said the king, "and you shall have good houses built for you in the court-yards of my palace."

The king and his parents and his sister then lived very happily together for the rest of their lives.

Koba, the Hunter
who stopped Hunting

There was once a man called Koba, a hunter. One day he left his house and went off to hunt in a place which was far away.

When Koba reached a certain locust-bean tree, he made his camp under it. Every day he went out hunting, and every night also, resting only for necessity, to eat and to sleep.

One day when he was out hunting he suddenly heard the mighty roar of a lion very close to him. Never had he heard such a roar before. Greatly alarmed, Koba turned and ran as fast as he could towards his camp. He was carrying a bow and some arrows. On the way his bow caught in the low branches of a tree. He pulled but could not release the bow, and he thought it was the lion who had caught it, but he was too frightened to turn his head to look.

"Please, King of Animals," cried Koba, "let go of my bow. I have not come out to hunt you. You are the king not only of animals but also of human beings who are your Majesty's subjects."

Koba never turned his head. He waited for an answer from the lion, but as it was branches of a tree holding his bow there was no answer.

"If you are angry with me because of other hunters," Koba continued, "I promise to tell them no longer to hunt you. If you are too angry to release my bow, keep it. Only let me go free to tell other hunters not to hunt lions."

Again there was no answer. Koba left his bow and ran on to his camp by the locust-bean tree. Quickly he packed his belongings, and then made the journey back to his house with all possible speed.

"My brothers!" Koba cried when he reached his house and found two of his friends, "I have a terrible story to tell you of my escape from a lion whose roar is greater than any thunder."

After he told them his story, the two friends said, "Lead us to the place where the lion caught your bow."

Koba led the two friends all the way back to the place. When they arrived, they saw the bow in the low branches of a tree.

"See," said Koba, "the lion must have given my bow to this tree in order to return it to me. The lion is not only the king of animals, but he is also the king of trees."

The two friends said that it was the branches of the tree which had caught the bow, not a lion.

"No, no," Koba declared. "It was certainly a lion. He pulled the bow and I pulled the bow, but the lion being stronger than me forced me to leave the bow with him."

From that day onwards, for the rest of his life, Koba never dared go far into the forest or the bush from his home. However much his two friends might laugh, he feared that he would meet a lion, and that the lion would remember his promise to tell all other hunters never to hunt lions again. Koba himself never hunted again: he became a farmer.

A Rich Man and his Goat

In a small town in the north there once lived a rich but foolish man whose name was Abdullahi. This rich and foolish man owned many sheep, many cattle, and many goats, but unfortunately Abdullahi had no sons and no daughters.

One day Abdullahi met the judge of the town.

"Because you have neither sons nor daughters," the judge of the town said to Abdullahi, "all your sheep, your cattle, and your goats will be given to the chief of the town when you die."

"Why is that?" Abdullahi asked.

"In this town," the judge replied, "that is the law."

Now Abdullahi was very angry when he heard this, because he did not want all his sheep, his cattle, and his many goats to be given to the chief of the town.

"I will sell my animals in the market," Abdullahi told his friends, "and I shall enjoy the money while I can."

When three rascals in the town heard what Abdullahi planned to do, they decided to play a trick on him and at the same time gain some advantage for themselves. When they saw Abdullahi go out of the town they greeted him. After greetings they asked where he was going.

"I am going to get one of my fat goats," Abdullahi told them. "I shall bring it to market and I shall sell it."

"We will be seeing you on your way back," the three rascals said.

After Abdullahi had gone, the rascals separated, each going to a different place beside the path where they waited for two hours.

After two hours had passed the first rascal saw Abdullahi on his way back, carrying a fat goat on his shoulder. The first rascal greeted Abdullahi very politely and humbly; then he said, as if he were saying a shameful thing, "It disappoints me, my friend, to see a gentleman like you carrying a pig, which is against our religion, instead of a goat."

Abdullahi was very surprised. He put his hand to his head.

"You cannot think I am carrying a pig," he said, and he went on his way.

Abdullahi had not gone far when he saw the second rascal sitting by the side of the path. The rascal was pretending to finger his string of beads and to pray. Abdullahi stopped to ask the pious man for his blessing.

"How can I bless you," the rascal said, "when you are carrying a pig?"

Abdullahi rubbed his eyes as if he were trying to see what was the truth. Without a word, but with a much troubled mind, he went on his way.

Abdullahi reached the third rascal, who also had a string of

prayer beads in his hand. The rascal stood up when he saw Abdullahi and stepped to one side to show his disapproval.

"You are doing strange things," he said to Abdullahi, and he spoke with a stern voice. "You told me you were going to get a goat and now you are carrying a pig."

"Is it really a pig?" the foolish Abdullahi asked, and the rascal told him it was.

"When you reach the market," said the rascal, "all the townspeople will be horrified that you are carrying a pig."

This was too much for Abdullahi. He threw down his goat, thinking it was a pig, and ran into the town. He went to the compound of the chief of the town, and as he went he told the townspeople what had happened.

"I am not well," Abdullahi cried when he and the townspeople came before the chief. He told the chief the story of what had happened.

But the chief and the townspeople understood how the foolish Abdullahi had been tricked out of his goat and they laughed and laughed at Abdullahi's great foolishness.

Meanwhile, the three rascals had caught the goat which Abdullahi had thrown down. They took it to another market and sold it, and then divided the money among themselves.

The Boy who had to choose his Father

Once upon a time there lived a very poor man and his son, who caught rats and sold them. They were so poor that if on any day they earned no money, they would have nothing to eat that day.

One day when the poor man and his son were hunting rats, they found a large hole. When the father started to dig into the hole, a large rat came out, which the father caught and gave to his son to hold. Then the father started to dig into the hole again. Another large rat ran out. The father chased it, but it escaped. While the father was chasing that rat, the other one jumped from the hands of the son and it too ran away.

"Now we have lost both rats," the father cried to his son. "The night is coming and it is too late to catch anything else. We have nothing to sell and no money. We have no light for night hunting. Because of your clumsiness we shall have nothing to eat." Saying this, the father took a stick and beat his son. He beat him until he seemed to be dead.

"It will be easier to feed only myself in the future," said the father to himself as he went away. "I shall not be troubled with such a clumsy, foolish son."

Soon after the father left his son there came on horseback a very rich man called Idirisu, the richest man in his town. Seeing the boy lying on the ground, he told his servants to help him, to pick him up, and to give him water. Soon the boy recovered.

"You shall come back to my town," the rich man said.

Putting a gown of cloth on the lad and setting him on his horse, the rich man continued his journey.

"You shall be my son," said Idirisu to the boy.

When the rich man reached his town, he went to his house and took the boy to live with him.

The people of the town were very surprised to see Idirisu, the rich man, with an almost full-grown boy whom the rich man said was his son.

"Where did you get this boy?" they asked him.

"He is my son," Idirisu answered.

"We all know," the people said, "that you have neither son nor daughter."

"My wife," said the rich man, "went back to her village when she gave birth to this child and he grew up with her. I have now brought him back to my house."

The people were not satisfied that this was true. However, the rich man treated the boy as if he really were his son. He gave him much money and many presents and bought him a splendid horse. He even found a girl to be a wife for him.

There were other rich men in the town who all had sons. They planned to test whether the boy who lived in Idirisu's house was really his son. They dressed their own sons in their most expensive clothes, gave money to each of them, and mounted them on valuable horses. The sons asked the boy from Idirisu's house to go outside the town, to go riding with them. He went, but not before Idirisu had quietly warned him, "Do just what all the others do."

Outside the town the rich men's sons did what their fathers had planned that they should do. They gave all their money away to beggars. The boy from Idirisu's house did the same. Then the rich men's sons took off their expensive gowns and threw them away, as well as their expensive caps and other clothing. The boy from Idirisu's house did the same. Then the rich men's sons dismounted and drove away their horses. The boy from Idirisu's house did likewise.

When they all returned to the town the rich men's sons told their fathers that the boy from Idirisu's house had given away his money, thrown away his expensive clothes, and had driven off his valuable horse, just as they had done.

"He must really be the rich Idirisu's son," they said at last.

The years passed, and every year Idirisu was like a father to the boy, doing the best that he could for him.

After many years the real father of the boy chanced to see his son out riding on a fine horse, outside the town. The father, who was still a very poor hunter of rats, recognized his son. When he asked about him, he heard that the young man was rich and was treated as the son of the rich Idirisu.

Going to the town, the father went to the house of the richest man, Idirisu. He saw his son and he saw how truly rich he had become.

"You are my son," said the man.

"Yes," said the son, "I am."

The son went immediately to Idirisu and told him that his real father had come to the house, whereupon Idirisu went to the father.

"Greetings to you, stranger," said Idirisu. "You may lodge here for the night."

The father was given a room in which to sleep; good food, and much of it, was sent to him.

During the night Idirisu went to the father; the father said that he had come to take away his son.

"If you leave your son with me," said Idirisu, "I will give you great wealth and anything you may ask."

"I want nothing," said the father, "except my son."

Idirisu thereupon became very angry. Calling the son, he told him that his real father wanted him back, but that he, Idirisu, wanted him to stay.

"Tomorrow we shall go out of the town," Idirisu declared. "We shall take a sword."

The next day the rich Idirisu, the poor father, and the son went outside the town. Idirisu took a sharp sword with him.

"Now decide," Idirisu said to the son, handing him the sword. "Either kill me and follow your father, or kill your father and follow me."

"I would rather kill myself," said the son, "instead of destroying either you or my father."

He raised the sword high above his head and threw it as far away as he was able. He then made his decision; it was a very wise one. Both Idirisu and the father were satisfied and so was the son.

Now, reader, if you were the son, what would you have done? What would have been your decision?

A Boastful Man who was not Brave

There lived a man called Sule who was a farmer. He was very conceited, and thought that he was better than other men. Every day when he returned to his house from the farm he would say to his wife, who was called Ladi, "Do you think there is any man in this district who is stronger or braver than I?"

"No," Ladi always replied in order to please her husband, "there is no one stronger or braver than you."

When Sule heard her reply, he was always delighted, and he would laugh with pleasure. But Ladi told her mother and father what Sule had been saying.

"He is foolish," Ladi's father said. "He should be taught that he is no stronger and no braver than any other man."

"Go," Ladi's mother advised, "go and tell Sule that you wish to visit your brother, who is of the same father and the same mother as yourself."

Ladi agreed to do this.

"Tell Sule," Ladi's mother went on, "that you are frightened to go by yourself to your brother's village because the path is through the forest. Ask him to go with you to protect you."

Ladi's mother then explained the plan which had come into her mind. After this Ladi went back to her husband's house. She said she wanted to visit her brother and asked Sule to go with her through the forest because she was too frightened to go alone.

"I shall go with you," Sule replied, "after one week has passed."

Ladi told her parents when she and Sule would be leaving.

Meanwhile, Ladi's parents told a powerful soldier to go to the forest, to pretend that he was going to kill Sule, so that Sule would have to prove whether or not he really was as strong and as brave as he said.

After one week had passed, Ladi and one of Ladi's sisters, together with Sule, started their journey through the forest. Ladi carried a gown, a blanket, and two white caps as presents for her brother. Sule carried a bow and arrows, and also carried a spear, a sword, and a big knife.

"I shall protect you," Sule said, "from any danger."

They walked and they walked for a very long time. When they reached a place where two paths crossed, Ladi led the way down the path where she knew the powerful soldier was waiting. Suddenly, when they reached a very large mahogany tree, the powerful soldier came out in front of them. He was wearing only a goat-skin and he carried a big wooden stick.

"Stop!" cried the powerful soldier, raising his big stick. "Where are you from and where are you going? Do you not know me? I am the King of the Forest."

With these words he strode towards Sule, Ladi, and Ladi's sister, pretending he was going to beat them. Ladi and her sister threw down what they were carrying and ran behind Sule. Sule threw down his bow and arrows, and also his spear, his sword, and his big knife, and started to run away.

"Stop!" cried the powerful soldier, catching hold of Sule. "I shall take away the two women and you I shall kill."

Then he said to Ladi, "What is your name?"

"My name is Ladi," she replied.

The powerful soldier put down his stick.

"Ladi!" he exclaimed. "That is the name of my mother. I could never hurt anyone with that name. Please forgive me."

He said to Ladi's sister, "What is *your* name?"

"My name is Ladi," she replied.

The powerful soldier said to *her* that he could never hurt her because she had his mother's name. He asked her also to forgive him.

Then the powerful soldier said to Sule, "What is *your* name?"

"My name," Sule replied, "is Ladi."

The powerful man looked at Sule and said in a terrible voice, "How could you have the name of a woman? You are a man."

"Truly," said Sule, "believe me that I am a woman."

When Sule said these words Ladi and her sister and the powerful soldier laughed and laughed. They laughed until they cried. Then they told Sule that they had tricked him. They returned to their village, and everyone in the village laughed at Sule.

After that, when anyone asked Sule who was the strongest and bravest of all the men in the district, Sule would reply, "I am the strongest and bravest man, but only in my own compound."

One day Sule sewed a penny on to his blanket as a decoration. That night he sat outside in the courtyard of the compound talking to his friends. They sat talking until it was late and the moon was high. When Sule went to lie down to sleep, he had forgotten about the penny sewn on to his blanket. As he wrapped the blanket around him he felt the coldness of the penny. Jumping up quickly, he cried, "Snake! Snake!"

Sule's friends came running to help, bringing sticks. They beat the blanket, but there was no snake. Then they saw the penny sewn on to the blanket. They laughed and laughed. They laughed until they cried. Then they told him that he had tricked himself.

"You are not the strongest and bravest man," they said to Sule, "not even in your own compound."

Now Sule became very ashamed. He went to his room, and while everyone was sleeping, he collected all his belongings and then went quietly out of the compound.

"I shall leave here for ever," said Sule to himself as he left the village, and he was never seen again in that district.

The Story of Ja'afaru
and his Mother's Sons

There was a certain man called Ja'afaru who lived in a large city. With him lived his brothers, the two other sons of his mother. Their father was a rich man and old.

One day their father became ill. Lying down, he called his sons to him and told them that he would soon die. After twelve days of illness he said, "Here is my house and here are my riches." Then he died.

Three days passed, and on the fourth day after the father had died the judge called the sons to him. Their names were taken, and it was proved that they were the sons of their rich father.

"I shall send my deputy," said the judge, "and he will divide your father's property and riches between you according to the law."

The sons returned to their father's compound, and the deputy of the judge went to the compound. He spoke to each of the sons and he inspected their father's property. He then divided the property between the sons and saw that each received his correct share. When he had finished he went away.

Two of the sons took their wealth and went out into the city. They hired drummers and singers to praise them. They bought wives, they bought rich clothes, they ate expensive food, and they drank wines which made them insensible. But the son called Ja'afaru did not waste his money, for he became a trader who worked hard and traded wisely. He gained profits from his trading and he increased his wealth.

Meanwhile, the two brothers had lost everything which they had received from their father. They went to Ja'afaru's house and saw how successfully he was trading.

"Ja'afaru, our brother," the two brothers said to him, "please lend us some money. We will buy and sell ground-nuts. We will return your money from the profit we will make."

Ja'afaru gave them the money.

The two brothers left the city at once and went to a near-by town. There they went to a house of gambling, and there they soon lost all the money which Ja'afaru had given them.

Then the two brothers went to the market-place. They begged for food, crying, "We are without even one-tenth of a penny. Please help to feed us."

Now the news of the two brothers reached Ja'afaru. He sent a messenger to them telling them to return. As the two brothers were coming up to the gates of the city, they were met by Ja'afaru's servants. The servants brought them fine clothes to wear and horses to ride. So the two brothers entered the city and went to Ja'afaru's house looking like rich men. The people of the city were respectful when they saw the brothers arriving as they did, and they said to each other, "See, the brothers of Ja'afaru. They went away to trade ground-nuts and they have returned in fine clothes and riding horses."

Ja'afaru greeted his brothers and made them rest and eat in his house. After they had rested and eaten for several days, Ja'afaru spoke with them.

"Tell me, my brothers," Ja'afaru asked, "what happened to the money which I lent you?"

"Ah," cried the first brother, "there was bad luck for me. When I left the city thieves attacked me. They came out from the bush. They wounded me. They stole all the money that you gave me."

"I bought many sacks of ground-nuts," said the second brother. "Unfortunately, there was a fire, and all the ground-nuts were burnt. Also burnt was some of the money which you gave me, that part of the money which had not been spent to buy the ground-nuts."

Ja'afaru was very sorry to hear what the brothers told him. He told them that he forgave them their debt and that they should remain in his house. The two brothers thanked Ja'afaru and went to the rooms he had given them.

A month passed, and the two brothers went to their brother and spoke to him.

"Ja'afaru," they said. "If you lend us some money, we will go and buy cotton. Then we will sell the cotton. We will return your money from the profit we will make."

Once more Ja'afaru gave them the money.

The two brothers left the city at once and went to a near-by village. There they bought wives and went to a house of gambling. They bought expensive food and they drank wine which made them insensible. They soon lost their money, but instead of begging, they stole. They stole money from a trader, but, alas! they were caught and bound with rope. The news was sent to Ja'afaru.

When Ja'afaru heard this story of his brothers he got up from the carpet on which he was sitting. He made arrangements to go on a journey. He left his house and went to the village where his brothers had been caught as thieves and had been bound with rope.

Ja'afaru went to the chief official, the Waziri. Touching the foot of the Waziri to show his respect, he gave money and presents to him. The Waziri agreed to release Ja'afaru's two brothers.

Once more Ja'afaru had fine clothing brought for his brothers and he mounted them on horses. Back they rode to the city, returning to Ja'afaru's house.

"We thank you, Ja'afaru," said the two brothers.

"You will never have to thank me again," said Ja'afaru. So saying, he took them into his house, where he continued to give them food and clothing, but never again would he give them money, not even a single tenth of a penny.

The Story of Mullum the Soldier

Long ago there lived a man called Mullum. He was a great soldier, and he was the leader of all the soldiers in his country. He was respected in his own country and he was feared in all the neighbouring countries.

One day Mullum went out hunting on his war horse, a black animal, and, like his master, very strong and brave. The war horse was also a great jumper, and could leap over rocks and streams. Mullum naturally valued him very much.

Now on the day that Mullum went hunting he saw no animals at all. Because of that he went farther and farther away from his town, and deeper and deeper into the forest. He went so deep into the forest that unknown to him he left his own country and went into the country of his enemies.

As he had travelled a long way, Mullum grew tired. Dismounting from his horse, he put a piece of rope between the horse's front legs so that it could not go far away. Then he lay down in the shade of a tree with many leaves and went to sleep.

It happened that some of the enemies of Mullum were also out hunting in the forest on that same day. Suddenly they saw Mullum's horse which had wandered away from its master while searching for green grass to eat. Seeing a horse with no one beside it, the men tried to catch it, but even with its front feet tied close together, the horse was too savage and strong for them, and the men hurried back to their town.

"Come quickly to the forest!" they cried when they saw their brothers in the town. "There is a very mighty black horse which we want to catch."

They returned to the forest with many of the bravest men of their town. There was a great fight, but at last the large number of men were able to catch the horse, and they led it back to their town, where it was taken to the palace of the king.

"May your life be long," the men with the horse greeted their king. "See, we have captured a fine black horse."

"I see it," said the king, "and I am overjoyed. This is the horse of Mullum, my enemy. Without his best horse, Mullum will not be able to fight so well."

The king gave orders that the horse should be tied up in the palace courtyard and be given freshly cut grass.

Now all this time, Mullum had been asleep. When he woke up, he could not find his horse. he looked all around him and he called, but in vain. Then he saw a man who was collecting wood.

"Greetings to you," said Mullum to the man who was collecting wood. "Have you seen my horse?"

The man had seen the horse being caught, but he did not like to say so. All he said was that he thought the horse had been taken to the near-by town. Mullum then realized that he was in the country of his enemies.

"Run to the town," Mullum ordered the man, "and tell the king that I am determined to search for my horse."

The man who had been collecting wood ran to the town and delivered the message. When the king heard the news he and several of his followers rode out to meet Mullum, whom they met walking along a path in the forest, on his way to their town. Mullum and the king greeted each other.

"Have you seen my horse?" Mullum asked.

"Perhaps," the king replied.

"Is my horse in your town?" Mullum asked.

"It may be," said the king.

Mullum demanded that his horse be returned.

"Be patient," said the king.

Mullum said he would go to the town to look. The king agreed, and they returned to the town.

"Here is a house for you to rest in," the king said to Mullum, "and here is fire and water and food. Sleep, for night is coming. Tomorrow we shall talk about the horse."

Mullum was unwilling to wait, but he knew that only by some trick, cunning, or good fortune would he and his horse be freed. He went into the house and found it comfortable. He tasted the food and found it good. He finished it, and then he lay down on his mat and went to sleep.

As Mullum slept, he dreamt that he saw a beautiful girl standing near him. He woke up from the dream and found that morning had come, and that there really was a beautiful girl standing near him.

"Who are you?" he asked her.

"I am a princess," she replied. "The king of this town is my father."

"Will you marry me?" Mullum asked her.

"Yes, if you ask my father's permission," said the princess, and she ran lightly away back to the king's palace.

Mullum went to see the king and asked for permission to marry the princess.

"I will give permission," said the king, "if you promise me that you will never fight against us again, and if war does arise between my country and the country of your king, you must let my daughter, the princess, return."

Mullum agreed to the king's conditions, and he also asked that his horse be given back to him.

"Take my daughter and take your horse," said the king. Mullum thanked the king. "Remember your promise to return my daughter if there is war," the king repeated.

Mullum left the town and went back through the forest to his own country, together with his horse and with the beautiful princess.

For half a year Mullum and the beautiful princess lived happily together. Then war began between the people of the princess's country and the people of Mullum's country. The father of the princess sent a message that she must be sent back to him without delay.

"I must go," said the princess to Mullum.

"Yes, it has been my promise," Mullum said. "Now there is war, so you must go back."

Preparations were made for the departure of the princess. Before she left, Mullum gave her a small square envelope made of leather which had been dyed red, and inside it was a magic charm.

"You will soon have a child," Mullum told the princess. "If you hang this leather envelope around the child's neck, there will be fame and fortune for the child during the child's life."

Mullum then said farewell to the princess, saying at the end, "If you give birth to a boy, I should like to know. Please send me a message."

The princess said she would do as she was asked. So saying, she started on her journey back through the forest to the town where her father was king.

The princess safely reached the town and the palace of her father the king, who welcomed her, and gave her a room of her own.

Not long afterwards the princess gave birth to a boy. Around his neck she hung the envelope of red leather which Mullum had given her so that there would be fame and fortune during his life. But the princess was deceitful, for she sent a message to Mullum saying that their child was a girl, and not a boy.

The child of the princess was given the name of Sahabi; he grew up to be strong and of good character.

"Tell me," he asked the princess, "who was my father?"

"He is still alive," the princess replied. "He is the chief of the soldiers in the next king's country and he is a famous fighter."

Sahabi himself was becoming well known as a fighter as he grew older, and he determined that he would go to the next king's country. He thought, "I shall conquer that country, and when I have done so, I shall make my father the king."

Sahabi made preparations for war, gathering soldiers about him. They went to the near-by kingdom, and after a battle they conquered that country. Sahabi captured that country's king.

"You are now my slave," said Sahabi to the captured king, "and I shall take you to show my father."

Before Sahabi could reach the town where his father lived, news reached the town that a strong young leader of soldiers from the country of their enemies had captured the king and was on his way to attack the town. It was Mullum who was chosen to lead the soldiers against the invaders. He had his famous black horse brought to him, and he called together his own soldiers.

The next day the two armies met. Mullum saw Sahabi and Sahabi saw Mullum, but they did not know that they were father and son. There was much fighting. The soldiers of one country fought the soldiers of the other country. Mullum and Sahabi fought each other. At the end of the day, all were weary, and each side withdrew to their camps for the night.

On the following day the armies approached each other again. Sahabi called to Mullum.

"Leader of the enemy," he called. "What is your name?"

Mullum would not answer, for he was proud. He did not wish to speak with the enemy. When the fighting started once more, Sahabi, with his growing strength, knocked Mullum from his horse (which had become old and slow) and was about to kill him.

"Let me rise and fight again," Mullum cried. "It is not bravery to kill a man at the first blow."

Sahabi allowed Mullum to rise from the ground, and the

fighting between them continued. Then Sahabi fell to the ground. Mullum drew his battle-axe and cut Sahabi across the chest.

"Alas," cried Sahabi. "All my attempts have failed. All my plans have been in vain. Now I am killed in battle in my search for my father Mullum."

At once Mullum realized that he had been fighting with his own son, and he saw for the first time around the neck of Sahabi the envelope of red leather which he had given to the princess for her child when she had gone back to her father.

Mullum sent a message to his own king asking for a special medicine that would help Sahabi, but the king refused, saying, "I will not try to save an enemy like Sahabi." When Sahabi died, his soldiers fled back into the forest from which they had come.

"Never shall I fight again," Mullum declared. "Through being a soldier I have lost my son."

And he lived as a peaceful man for the rest of his life.

The Story of a Princess
and Two Princes

Long ago there was a handsome prince and a young princess, both of whom lived in the same town.

The father of the princess and the father of the prince arranged that the handsome prince and the young princess should be married. There was feasting, dancing, and drumming after the marriage ceremony. After the wedding, the handsome prince bought a strong white horse which he called Kili.

The prince was very fond of his white horse, and he would say to him, "Kili, Kili. You are better than a wife."

Now the young princess heard her handsome prince saying to his horse, "Kili, Kili. You are better than a wife." She became very angry. She became very jealous.

"I hate your horse Kili," the young princess said to her husband. "If you wish me to obey you in everything, you must kill your white horse."

"Never," said the handsome prince. "I shall never kill Kili."

It happened that another handsome prince in another town heard the story. He also had a strong white horse, and this horse was also called Kili. The rival prince put on his finest clothes, his shining black turban, and his large, hand-worked gown. Mounting his white horse, he rode to the town of the other handsome prince.

He soon reached his compound, but found that the prince was away. From the compound he went into a courtyard, and from there into the house of the young princess. But he left his own white horse outside, and instead led in the other prince's white horse.

The young princess and the newly arrived handsome prince greeted each other. Then said the handsome prince, "I have heard that you and your prince are quarrelling. Perhaps you will marry me instead of him."

"I will not marry you," she answered, "because you have a white horse called Kili and you will prefer him to me."

"My white horse is nothing to me compared with you," said the prince. So saying, he drew his sword from its silver scabbard and killed the other handsome prince's white horse.

"You see," he cried. "I have proved that I prefer you to my horse."

The prince then left the compound and returned to his town, taking with him his own white horse which he had left waiting outside.

When the prince, who had been away, came back to his young princess and to his compound, he found that his white horse Kili had been killed. He was naturally very angry, and questioned the servants in the compound. He questioned the young princess, and asked if she had caused Kili to be slain.

"I did not kill your horse," she replied, "but because you cared more for your horse than for me, I shall follow another prince."

The young princess had her belongings packed, and off she went, following the road along which the other prince had gone.

Thus the handsome prince had lost both his white horse and his young princess.

The Marriage of the Hunter's Sister

There was once a brave and successful hunter. His name was Obian. He lived in the forests near the place where a river joined the sea. He had guns and with them he shot a great many animals.

Whenever an animal saw the hunter, it fled as fast as it could. But the hunter was skilful and he still caught many animals.

Finally, the animals of the forests gathered together and held a meeting. They decided that they would take revenge on the hunter.

"I am the king of beasts," said the lion. "I will take vengeance on this fearsome hunter."

So the lion changed himself into a well-dressed man and put money in his pocket. Then he went to the village where the hunter lived. In the centre of the village, where there was an open space, he saw some pretty girls. They were playing, laughing and singing. The lion knew that one of them was the hunter's sister. He looked at her and she looked at him. They talked together. She told him her name was Kariba. Finally he said to her, "Will you marry me?"

"Perhaps," Kariba answered, "but we must go and consult my parents."

They went to the house of Kariba's parents. The lion dressed as a man was so pleasing in his appearance and seemed to have so much money that the parents agreed to the marriage.

"The marriage ceremony will take place as soon as possible," said Kariba's father to the lion dressed as a man.

It was also arranged that the newly married couple would

leave the village immediately afterwards. It was then that Obian, the hunter, who had been away in the forest with his gun, returned to the village and to the house. He was told what had happened.

Now the hunter was very wise in the ways of the forest. He realized that it was no man who wanted to marry his sister. He knew it was the lion.

"This is not a man, it is a lion," Obian warned Kariba. "It is not wise to marry him."

"I do not believe you," she answered angrily. "I want to be married. Can you suggest anyone else for me?"

The hunter left his sister and before the lion could see him, he returned to the forest. He went quickly and secretly to the place where he knew the lion lived. There he waited.

In the village, meanwhile, there was much celebration. There was music, drumming and dancing. There was so much to eat and drink that everyone was more than satisfied. Kariba and the lion in human shape were married.

"Now we must go," said the bridegroom to his bride. He left the village on the path into the forest and she followed him.

After they had travelled for about five miles, Kariba was tired and asked her new husband how far away he lived.

"We are very close," he replied. "Let us walk faster."

As they came near the cave where he lived, his appearance began to change. His legs became those of a lion, then his body, then his head. He changed entirely into the lion which he really was.

"We have come to my home," roared the lion, running and jumping around Kariba. "Now I shall eat you."

The girl could not speak or cry out, she was so frightened. She did not know that her brother Obian, the hunter, was nearby.

"You will be my food and this will punish the hunter for shooting animals," the lion cried, preparing to kill the girl by jumping on her.

Suddenly they heard the shot of a gun. The lion was not hit but he became very frightened. Before the gun could be fired again, the lion turned and ran swiftly away. He disappeared in the forest.

"Here I am, your brother who came to save you," cried Obian, as he came from behind the trees. "Let us escape."

"Yes, yes," Kariba cried. "Let us run home."

As they ran, the day was turning to night. They reached their village in darkness and told their story. All night the villagers kept fires burning and beat drums to frighten away the lion in case he tried to return.

The next day the villagers all met together with Obian, the hunter, and Kariba, his sister.

"Let this be a warning," Kariba's father announced to the people. "Let none of our daughters ever marry unknown strangers who come to our village."

Everyone agreed with these words. Then Obian stood up to speak.

"Every man must take his gun and enter the forest; we will chase all lions and finish with them for ever."

The lion who had changed himself into a man was watching, hidden in the high grass nearby. When he heard Obian's words and saw every man collect his gun, he ran swiftly away. He warned all the lions and they fled for ever from that part of the country.

How the Cat destroyed the Rats

Once upon a time there was an old woman who was very much troubled by the large number of rats in her house. The rats chewed the mats, the clothes, the baskets. They gnawed at everything. They even ate her food. At last the old woman could bear it no longer.

"I shall leave this house," she said to herself. She moved to a lonely plain several miles away from the village, but the rats followed her there.

One day the old woman was sitting beside her hut, which she had made for herself in the lonely plain, when suddenly she saw an enormous cock jumping and running towards her. The nearer the cock came to the old woman the more she became afraid, for she had never before seen such a large fowl.

"Good-day, old woman," said the cock and the old woman returned his greeting.

"Why are you living alone in this plain?" the cock asked her.

She told him about her trouble with the rats, first in her house in the village and then out in the lonely plain.

"I can help you," said the cock.

"Ah, yes, but what reward do you want?" asked the old woman.

"Just a handful of corn every hour."

Instead of giving the cock a handful of corn every hour, the old woman was foolish enough to fill a large basket with corn and put it outside her hut.

As soon as the old woman had gone inside the hut, the cock ate all the corn and then continued on his way.

When the old woman discovered that the corn and the cock were gone and nothing had been done about the rats, she was very angry; but there was nothing she could do. She sat down on the ground outside her hut once again. Then she saw coming towards her a very small cat. It was no bigger than a rat.

"Good-day, little cat," said the old woman, and the cat returned the greeting.

The old woman told the cat about her trouble with the rats, first in her house in the village and then out in the lonely plain.

"I can help you," said the cat.

"Yes, but what reward do you want?" asked the old woman.

"I want nothing unless I first get rid of the rats."

"Now go to the market," said the cat to the old woman, "and buy some locust bean cakes which you must grind. Then cover my whole body with the ground beans."

Off to market went the old woman, where she bought the locust bean cakes. Returning to her hut, she ground the cakes to a powder and covered every inch of the cat's body with the

ground-up cakes. The cat crept quietly up to the rats' hole, lay down on the ground and pretended to be dead.

In the evening, when the rats were beginning to come out from their hole, they saw the cat looking as if he were dead. They ran off to tell the King of Rats.

"We must celebrate the death of the cat," declared the King of Rats. He commanded all the rats to join him for dancing and drumming.

They were all dancing, singing and beating their drums around the cat that night, when suddenly he sprang up. He jumped on the head of the King of Rats and ate him up. Then the cat, small as he was, turned and attacked all the other rats. Quickly, he ate them all up too. Yet there was no change in his shape, for he was a magic cat.

The old woman was at last freed of her troubles.

"Thank you, good cat," she said. "Now what reward shall I give you?"

"My reward is inside me," the cat replied. "My reward has been your rats."

A Good Fortune in Camels

Ali was a man who longed to go out into the world to see strange lands and seek his fortune.

He said to his wife, "Tomorrow I shall go out into the world."

She did not want him to go, but she was too wise to try to stop him.

The next morning, Ali set out on foot and walked until he found someone who would employ him for a short time. From that job he went to find another and then another, and so on until he had visited many strange lands. Of the money that he earned, he spent one-third on food and saved the other two-thirds. At last his thrift was rewarded and he was able to buy three camels with his savings.

As Ali was walking along with his three camels, he met another traveller.

"Greetings," said the traveller.

"Greetings to you," Ali answered.

They told each other where they came from and then the traveller said, "If you give me a present, I shall tell you something of value."

Ali gave the traveller one of the three camels.

"Do not go across any river which you do not know," said the traveller. "Wait until someone else goes first."

The man thanked the traveller, saying he was grateful for the advice. After going a short way, Ali met another traveller. They also greeted each other, and then the second traveller said, "If you give me a present, I shall tell you something of value."

Ali gave the traveller one of the two remaining camels.

"Do not rest," the traveller warned, "under a tree which has a big hole in it."

Ali thanked him, saying he was grateful for the advice. When Ali continued his journey, he met a young boy. After they had greeted each other the young boy said, "If you give me a present, I shall tell you something of value."

So Ali gave the young boy his last camel.

"Be patient," said the boy. "Do not show your first feelings of anger."

Ali thanked him, saying he was grateful for the advice. They parted and Ali, with no more camels, went on his way. He had not gone far before he met two camel drivers with thirty camels.

"Please help us with our camels," the camel drivers asked Ali, "so that each of us will have ten camels to lead."

Ali agreed and the three of them set off together with the camels. They came to a river which had flooded the fields on each side of its banks. The first camel driver took off his clothes and entered the water to look for the crossing. He fell into a deep part of the river and was not seen again. So the second camel driver and Ali did not cross there, but went on and found a safe crossing.

On the other side of the river they came to a forest. By that time the sun was setting and the men were tired. They looked for suitable trees to shelter them for the night. The camel driver took his sleeping mat and put it under a tree with a big hole in it. But Ali remembered the advice he had received and he moved away from that tree. In the middle of the night, a large snake came out of the hole in the tree and killed the sleeping camel driver.

When daybreak came, Ali saw what had happened. He was very sad and sorry for the two camel drivers. He set out and asked everyone he met if they knew where the camel drivers lived. He wanted to return the camels to their families. But no one could tell him and he lost patience. He controlled his anger, however. In time he realized that no one knew where the camel drivers had lived.

So Ali collected the thirty camels and went back to his own part of the country, to his home and to his wife. She was over-joyed to see him.

"You have not only seen much of the world," said his wife, "but you have returned safely."

"Yes," Ali replied, "and my good fortune in camels will bring us riches for the rest of our lives."

The Fisherman and the Ring

A long time ago there lived a young man whose father was a teacher.

"I wish to be a fisherman," said the young man to his father. The father protested, for he thought that his son would not make much money nor become well known. But when he saw that his son was determined, he reluctantly gave him his blessing.

Thereupon the young man bought nets and all the equipment that fishermen need. Then he built himself a hut by the river. At first he caught few fish, but with practice he became more successful and caught many more. The young man sold his fish in the market and gave the money to his father.

Then war came to that district.

"Help to defend our people," said the teacher to his son. So the young man left his fishing, took up his bow, his arrows and his spear and successfully fought the marauding enemies. By the time the fighting was over, there had been many losses in the village. But the young man survived and he returned to the river and became a fisherman again.

One day the son was in his canoe on the river when he saw a movement on the surface of the water. Quickly he threw his net and caught a fish that was bright red. To his surprise, the fish spoke to him, for no fish had ever spoken to him before.

"Do not kill me," begged the fish.

"All right," said the fisherman. "Just this once I will let you go."

"Thank you," said the fish. "For your kindness you deserve a reward."

"I should like money," said the fisherman, putting the fish back into the river.

The fish swam away, returning after a short time with a ring in his mouth.

"Take this ring," said the fish. "You can buy anything you want with what the ring gives you."

With trembling hands the fisherman took the red fish's ring. Excitedly he returned to the shore and rushed into his hut by the river bank. After closing the door, he turned the ring in his hand and said, "Please may I have money to buy a new boat?" Money appeared before him.

"May I have some to give to my father?" More money appeared before him. The fisherman ran back to his village and to his father. He became the richest man in that village and the last days of the old teacher's life were happy because his son had become so successful.

Then war came again to that district. The village was attacked. During the fighting the fisherman called to his ring, "Oh, ring, turn our village which they are attacking into the place of destruction for our enemies. Turn our attackers into stone."

Immediately the enemy were turned into a mountain which one can see behind the village. To this day the villagers speak of the fisherman, the talking fish and his magic ring.

The Magic Crocodile

There was once a very big cave. It was divided into two parts, the top part being dry and the bottom part filled with water. In the bottom part there lived a crocodile.

The crocodile did not live alone in the cave, for various other wild animals stayed there too. They lived in the dry part and various water creatures swam in the part which was filled with water. The crocodile spent most of his time in the water, but sometimes he would emerge from the cave for a short distance.

One day a hunter went near the cave in search of animals. He saw the crocodile resting in the sunshine outside the mouth of the cave. The hunter aimed his bow and arrow at the crocodile but immediately his eyes became blind.

When the hunter let the arrow fall from the bow his eyes opened again. He could see the crocodile smiling with pleasure at the cleverness of his trick.

The hunter did not stay, but ran back to his village and told the people what had happened.

"As I pointed my arrow at the crocodile," the hunter declared, "I became blind. The arrow fell out of my bow and then I could see again."

The people in the village grew very excited. Nearly half of them took up their bows and arrows and went off towards the cave.

"We shall catch that crocodile," they all shouted.

When the villagers came near the cave they saw the crocodile where the hunter had seen it, resting in the sunshine outside the cave. The very moment that each villager put an arrow in his bow and aimed at the crocodile, he became blind.

"Take your arrows from your bows," cried the hunter, and when they did so, the eyes of the villagers could see again.

"No man can harm me," said the crocodile, looking at the villagers. He got up from his resting-place and went back into the cave where all the animals praised him for guarding them so well.

"We will live our own lives in our village," declared the disappointed villagers as they returned to their homes. "That crocodile will remain in his cave. There is nothing we can do to change this."

However, some of the young men were not satisfied with this. From time to time, an exceptionally brave youth would return to the cave determined to kill the crocodile. But he never succeeded.

"Be blind with your bows and arrows," said the crocodile with a smile. Neither he nor the villagers had ever seen or heard of guns in those days long ago.

The Contest between Fire and Rain

Once upon a time there was a king who had a beautiful daughter. Her beauty increased as she grew to the age of marriage and she was considered to be the most beautiful girl in the world.

Many men wanted to marry the king's daughter, but the first two to ask for her in marriage were Fire and Rain.

Rain went first to the king's daughter to ask if she would marry him, and she agreed; but Fire had gone first to the king

to ask to be allowed to marry his daughter, and the king had agreed.

The king sent word that his daughter was to come to see him.

"I have promised to give you in marriage to Fire," the king told her when she came into his room.

"Your Majesty," the king's daughter replied, "but I have already promised to marry Rain."

"What shall we do?" cried the king and his daughter. "We are caught between two promises."

It was then that Rain arrived in order to visit the king's daughter; soon after that Fire arrived with the same intention. Rain and Fire were each determined to outwit the other.

Then the king said, "I have decided on the day of marriage for my daughter."

"To me?" asked Fire.

"To me?" asked Rain.

"To the winner of a race on the day of the marriage," said the king. "To him I will give my daughter."

There was great excitement amongst the people. Some said Fire would win; others said Rain would win. The king's daughter said to herself that whoever won the race, she would keep her promise to marry Rain.

When the day came for the race and for the marriage, it was very windy. The king made a sign and a drum was beaten. The race began. At first Fire was winning, for he was carried rapidly along by the wind. As for Rain, there was no sign of him in the sky. Fire continued to race faster and faster until it seemed to everyone that he would certainly win. When Fire had almost reached the place where the king sat with his daughter, Rain was at last seen preparing himself in the sky. It seemed to everyone, however, that he was too late. But when Fire was just about to win the race, Rain started to fall very heavily. Fire was quenched before he could reach the end of the race and Rain was declared the winner.

The king therefore gave his daughter to Rain to be his wife and there was much rejoicing.

Ever since that time when water quenched flames, there has been enmity between Rain and Fire.

The Wise Old Man
and the Ferocious Leopard

This is an old story about a very ferocious leopard. At night he would come near the village huts where people lived. Any man, woman or child whom the leopard saw would be attacked. Even to leave their hut for a few minutes was impossible during the night, unless they were accompanied by men with flaming torches.

The leopard grew steadily bolder until at last he would force his way through the grass roofing of the huts and attack an entire family. Finally, those people who had donkeys or horses packed up their belongings and left the village and went to live elsewhere. But there were still many old people, poor people, and children who were left to the mercy of the leopard.

At last one old and experienced man went to each family.

"Buy knives," he advised them, "and collect firewood."

The people went to the nearest town and bought knives and they also collected bundles of firewood which the women brought back to the huts.

"Build fires in your huts at night," advised the old man, "and heat your knives."

That night they all built fires in their huts and heated the knives until they were red hot.

In the middle of the night the leopard arrived. He went first to the chief's hut but when he saw the fire, he crept away. He went to the next hut and to the next until he had been near every hut. But at each hut the sight of the fire made him turn

away. He was preparing to leave the village when his hunger drove him back.

The leopard approached the hut of the old man. He was the one who had advised the people to buy knives and collect firewood in order to light fires and to heat their knives.

The leopard jumped on to the roof of the hut and began to tear a hole in the grass.

"Here is our enemy the leopard," cried the old man to his family. "Help me pile stones."

The old man and his family piled stones for him to stand on. As the leopard forced his way through the grass roof so that he could jump into the hut, the old man seized his red-hot knife from the fire. He plunged the knife into the leopard, again and again.

"Now the leopard will no longer attack us," cried the old man. "He is dead and we can live without fear, and sleep peacefully in our huts at night."

So the people of that village decided that the old man should be their chief because of his wisdom and his bravery.

A Father's Warning

There was once a man and his son who always went hunting together. When they went hunting, the women in their compound kept all the dogs and horses tied up. The only animals not tied up were the horses on which the man and his son were riding.

One day, while out hunting, the man and his son met a strange woman. Her body was covered with a great many mouths, and she was cooking food in a large pot. As she cooked she fed the mouths. The air was filled with complaints from the impatient mouths: "Feed me." "Feed me." "I haven't had enough food." "Feed me."

When the man and his son saw this sight, the son called out, "Oh, what a terrible woman. What a terrible sight!"

The woman became very angry. She rushed at the man and his son, but they fled from her. Thereupon she changed herself, she and her many mouths, into many fast-flying birds. But the man and his son changed themselves into even faster flying birds. They flew back to the safety of their family home.

The strange woman was still angry, but she had a plan. She changed herself into a beautiful girl, more beautiful than any other girl in that country. Then she went to the village of the man and his son, carrying a large basket on her head.

In front of the chief's house the strange woman in the form of a beautiful girl called together all the young men of the village. She placed her large basket on the ground.

"Throw stones," she told the young men. "Whoever succeeds in knocking over the basket will be allowed to marry me."

All the young men wanted to marry the beautiful girl and so each one threw stones at the basket as best he could.

"Don't enter this competition," the hunter advised his son. "There is some hidden wickedness here."

But the son ignored his father's advice. Unlike the other young men who threw large stones, he threw a small stone at the basket. Immediately the basket fell over. The young man was therefore declared the winner of the contest. He was married to the beautiful girl and they lived in his family's compound.

After some days the beautiful girl said that she wanted her husband to take her back for a visit to her own village. The young man agreed.

"Tie up all the animals," the young man told the women in the compound. "But if the dogs cry, release them."

The young man mounted a handsome horse. Then he and his wife travelled to his wife's village. They arrived before dark and the young man was given a place to sleep.

In the middle of the night the young man was woken up. The leg of a man came up from under his bed.

"Go. Go," warned the leg. "Otherwise you will lose your life."

Without waiting for anything, the young man jumped up, ran to his horse, mounted and began to ride off.

The wife heard the young man leaving. She ran after him.

"Come back! Come back!" she shouted, but the young man paid no attention.

Quickly the beautiful girl changed herself into a mighty bird. She flew after the young man and his horse. She turned herself into the strange woman again, with the many hungry mouths all over her body. She pulled off one of the legs of the horse and she ate it. Then she pulled off another leg of the horse and she ate that too. Yet the remarkable horse was still running and carrying the young man on its back. The strange woman came again and again, until she had eaten the four legs and the body of the horse. Because there was nothing left for the young man to ride he quickly climbed up a tall tree.

The strange woman waited under the tree.

"When you come down from the tree we will eat you," cried the woman, "I and my many mouths."

"Yes. We will eat you," cried all the mouths.

Meanwhile, the dogs tied up at the young man's home began to howl and cry. The women in the compound remembered their instructions. They untied the dogs. The dogs rushed out. They found the tree with their master, the young man, clinging to its branches. Then they saw the strange woman beneath the tree and attacked her. They totally consumed every part of her, that strange woman and all her protesting mouths.

The young man came down from the tree. He gasped with relief and thankfulness for his escape. Then he saw his horse waiting for him, complete with its four legs and its body. He mounted the horse, and followed by his dogs, he returned home.

"You did well to release the dogs when they cried," he told the women in the compound. He provided them with a feast of goats, chickens and rice for them to eat and enjoy.

"You were right to warn me," he said to his father. "I know that in future I should follow your advice."

The Lion is not the King of Men

Once upon a time the lion summoned all the wild animals to his palace.

"Long may you live, and greetings," said the animals when they were all assembled.

The lion acknowledged their greetings and said, "I have called you here so that we may plan how best to combat the cruelties and injustices of men against animals."

After some discussion, the elephant suggested that they should start a school so that the young animals could be taught everything their elders knew.

"Which one of us," the lion asked, "would be the best teacher?"

"I will be their teacher," said the hyena.

The lion asked the hyena what he would teach the young animals.

"I would teach them to open their mouths very wide," said the hyena, "so that they might howl and show their teeth. The men who hunt us would become very frightened."

But the hare objected. He complained that small creatures like himself would not be able to frighten men in that way. The hyena could offer no arguments against this.

"Let us teach the young animals to hide in the grass beside bad smelling things," the hare suggested.

The elephant laughed at the hare.

"You poor little creature," she said, "how can you expect *me* to hide like that?"

All the animals laughed at the hare's suggestion.

"I will be the teacher," said the jackal.

The lion asked the jackal what he would teach the young animals.

"I would teach three things from my own behaviour," said the jackal. "When I search for food I always consider whether the food I see is in such places as might properly be expected. In that way I am not caught by traps."

The animals nodded their heads at this wisdom.

"Secondly," continued the jackal, "when I go to a pool or a stream to drink I look to see if anyone is near. Even if no one is near I still do not bend my head to the water."

The hare asked how he was able to drink.

"I put my tail in the water," replied the jackal. "Then I go a short distance away and suck the water from my tail. I repeat this until my thirst is satisfied."

The hyena asked how the jackal slept at night.

"I am coming to that," the jackal replied.

"Tell us quickly," ordered the lion.

"At night," the jackal continued, "I always cry out from one place and then go to another. Then amongst trees and bushes which are close together and where the leaves are very dry I go to sleep. If anything steps on the dry leaves, I hear the noise in time to wake up and run away."

All the animals praised the jackal for his wisdom.

"Jackal," declared the lion, "you shall be the teacher of our young animals."

The young animals were brought together to a school and they all paid attention to the lessons of the jackal, all except the lion cub.

"What is a mere man?" the lion cub would ask. "I hope one day to meet a man and kill him by scratching his body with my sharp claws."

One day the lion cub and a small hare went walking together after they had finished school. Suddenly they saw a man approaching. The lion cub stood still watching, not knowing that it was a man.

"What a strange creature," the lion cub thought.

When the man reached the lion cub, the man knelt on the

ground and greeted the lion cub with the politeness animals show towards lions.

"You are very different in appearance from other animals," said the lion cub. "Why have I never seen you at my father's palace?"

The man answered respectfully, "I do not go to the palace to greet your father the lion because I am ashamed. Unlike other animals, I haven't got much hair and I haven't a tail."

The lion cub then ordered the man to make a grass hut for him.

"I need protection from the sun," said the lion cub.

The man agreed and made a good, strong hut of sticks and ropes. The young hare who had been with the lion cub did not help, because he had run away.

"Please enter the hut, honoured lion cub," suggested the man. "See whether you find it comfortable."

When the lion cub had gone into the hut he told the man to close the door. The man did so, then started collecting twigs, leaves and grass which he piled around the sides of the hut. Then he set fire to the grass and the hut started to burn.

"Oh, hairless creature," cried the lion cub, "open the door and save my life."

"Today, boastful lion cub," replied the man, "you have met a man. Do I see you killing me with your claws? Instead you are in my power."

"I was wrong, I was wrong," the lion cub cried. "I apologize for my foolishness. I beg you to release me."

"Very well," the man agreed, opening the door of the burning hut and allowing the lion cub to escape from the flames. "Only remember, lions may be the kings of animals; but lions are not the kings of men."

The Hare and the Crownbird

One day the hare and his friend the crownbird went together on a journey. They were going to visit the house of the hare's uncle.

They travelled over hills and through valleys, until they came to a river. Beside the river there was an old woman washing herself.

"Please," the old woman asked the hare, "help me to wash my back."

"I will not," the hare replied.

Then the old woman saw the crownbird who was following the hare. "Please," the old woman asked the crownbird, "help me to wash my back."

"Yes, I will," the crownbird replied and began to help the old woman.

"Why do you bother yourself on such a task?" the hare said to the crownbird. "I will leave you to do this unrewarding job."

So saying, the hare continued on his journey.

After the crownbird had finished helping the old woman, she said to him, "Dip your wings and your legs into the water of this river."

The crownbird did so. Then the old woman told him to remove his wings and legs from the water. He did so. On his legs he discovered bracelets of great value and on the tips of his wings there were precious rings.

"Dip your beak into the water of this river," said the old woman.

The crownbird did so, and when the old woman told him to bring out his beak, he brought out beautiful clothing made of finely woven wool.

"Now once again," the old woman said. "Dip your wings into the water of this river."

Again the crownbird did as he was told, and bringing out his wings at the old woman's command, he found a very beautiful horse standing beside him.

"The bracelets, the rings, the clothing, the horse—all are for you," said the old woman to the crownbird. "I am grateful for the way you behaved when I asked you for help."

The happy crownbird mounted his new horse. It was a fast one and they soon caught up with the hare.

"How amazing," cried the hare. "You have bracelets, rings and fine clothes and you are riding a beautiful horse."

"Yes," replied the crownbird, "all this because of the old woman by the river."

Then he told the hare what had happened.

"Continue on your journey," the hare cried. "I'm going back to that old woman."

So he turned and ran off in the direction of the river.

When the hare reached the river, the old woman was still there. "Please let me help you," he said, smiling at her.

"Shall I take another bath?" the old woman asked angrily. "Shall I ask you again if you will help wash my back?"

"Yes, yes," cried the hare. "I will very willingly help you."

At first the old woman refused to be helped, but then because the hare continued to beg her to let him help she agreed. When the hare had finished helping her, she told him to put his legs and paws in the water of the river. The hare did so. When he withdrew them, they were covered with old and dirty bracelets and broken rings.

"Try again," said the old woman. But when the hare again withdrew his paws from the water of the river he held old and dirty clothing.

"Try again," repeated the old woman. But when for the third time the hare withdrew his paws from the water, he brought out the worst of all, a horse which was very ugly, short and thin.

The hare, with his dirty old bracelets, rings and clothing, mounted on his worthless horse and continued on his journey. The horse moved very slowly. Goats move better than that horse. Night had fallen by the time the hare reached his friend the crownbird at the house of the hare's uncle.

"I have learnt my lesson," the hare admitted. "It is better to give help than to refuse."

The Forgiving Wife

Okeke was a trader. Every day he would visit markets to buy goods which he would later sell.

Now Okeke had a neighbour who was also a trader. This neighbour enjoyed playing tricks and was deceitful.

One day the neighbour returned from the market before Okeke. He went to Okeke's house. Okeke's wife, whose name was Ugbala, thought she heard her husband coming and put out bowls of food. The neighbour quickly ate the food and then went away to his own house.

"Where is my meal?" Okeke asked when he returned home.

Ugbala said she had already brought out bowls full of food. Okeke and his wife then argued and quarrelled.

The next day the neighbour again returned early and went to Okeke's house. Again Okeke's wife thought she heard her husband and brought bowls of food. The neighbour quickly ate the food, as he had done the day before, and then went away to his own house.

"Where is my meal?" Okeke demanded when later he returned home.

Ugbala protested that she had already brought it to him. Again there was disagreement between them.

On the third day, Okeke's neighbour once more returned from market early and went to Okeke's house. Again he ate the food which Okeke's wife had prepared, and then went away. When Okeke came home to find his wife still insisting that she had already fed him, Okeke became very angry.

"I'll send you away, you troublesome woman," Okeke declared.

He gathered together the clothing and the shoes Ugbala had worn at their wedding. He threw the clothing and the shoes into a small canoe. Then he put his wife into the canoe and pushed it out into the river. The river was in flood and the water was moving very fast. The canoe quickly floated away.

Many miles down the river some fishermen were mending their nets. They looked up at the canoe and Ugbala saw them. She cried out for help and the fishermen were able to seize the canoe. They rescued the wife with her wedding clothing and her shoes.

"You are a fine woman," said one of the men. "Will you stay here and marry me?"

"No," Okeke's wife replied. "I shall go back to the land where I was born. I shall return to my father's house."

Ugbala set off on her journey with her belongings. She walked many miles. Finally, she reached her own country and her father's house.

"I wish to be a trader," she told her father. Now her father was a rich man and so he gave her money. She bought goods in one place and sold them in another, and as she always made a profit it was not long before she too became rich.

Meanwhile Okeke had not been successful in his trading. He was forced to borrow from his neighbours, but still he was unsuccessful. To settle the debts, the neighbours took Okeke's house and Okeke lost all that he had. He still went from market to market. He no longer went as a trader, however, but as a beggar.

One day Okeke reached the market near Ugbala's home. She saw him begging for food to eat. His clothing was ragged and his body was dirty. She sent a servant to bring him to her. The servant brought Okeke, but he did not recognize her.

"Take care of this man," Ugbala told her servant. "Bring him water for a bath. Call a barber to cut his hair. Give him new clothing and whatever he wants to eat and drink. Let him rest and sleep on a good bed."

The servant did all these things for Okeke.

Then Okeke's wife put on her wedding clothes and shoes. As she walked near Okeke the shoes began to sing: "Ugbala and Okeke. Ugbala and Okeke."

Okeke began to weep.

"Where did you get those shoes?" he cried.

"They are mine," replied Ugbala. "I am the wife you pushed away at the river side. Now you see I am alive."

Okeke became very frightened, and truly he had been regretting for a long time what he had done.

"Don't be afraid," said Ugbala. "I'm rich. I still want you to stay here as my husband."

Okeke stayed. From that day he and Ugbala were happy together, and he became a successful trader once again.

The Medicine for Getting a Son

A man named Obi and his wife Ngozi regretted that they had no child, for they had been married for many years. Finally, Obi went to a wizard to ask for his advice.

"Go," said the wizard, "and bring me the milk of a buffalo, the tears of an elephant, the tooth of a lion, the tail of a monkey and the brains of a lion."

Obi left his wife at home and started out in search of all these things the wizard had named. On his way he met a rabbit. He told the rabbit that he needed the milk of a buffalo.

"I will help you," said the rabbit, and went without delay to a buffalo he knew.

"Honoured buffalo," said the rabbit, "see if you can run like me through the thick bushes which you see there."

The rabbit ran up and down making a lot of dust, and jumped right over the thick bushes, but the buffalo did not realise this. He crashed into the thick bushes where his horns became stuck. Whatever he did he could not free himself. The rabbit waved to Obi, who came and milked the trapped buffalo.

Obi continued his journey. He had not been going long when he found an elephant weeping for the death of his son. Obi again asked the rabbit to help him. The rabbit readily agreed and ran up to the elephant saying, "Honoured elephant, the tears of a prince should not fall on the ground."

So saying, the rabbit held a bowl to the elephant's eyes and collected the tears. He carried the bowl to Obi.

Obi told the rabbit that he still needed the tooth of a lion and the tail of a monkey. The rabbit ran back to the elephant saying,

"The lions and the monkeys are laughing because you are weeping."

His words made the elephant very angry. He marched quickly up to a lion who lived nearby and attacked him, but he only succeeded in breaking one of the lion's teeth before the lion ran away. Then the elephant saw some monkeys and before they could run away too he had pulled off one of their tails with his powerful trunk. The rabbit, however, begged the elephant to give him the broken tooth and the tail. The elephant agreed and the rabbit returned to Obi.

"Here is a lion's tooth," said the rabbit, "and here is a monkey's tail. Now I must go about my own business."

Obi thanked the rabbit for his great help, and he and the rabbit parted. While Obi was wondering how he might obtain the brains of a lion, a donkey passed by. Obi decided to follow the donkey to ask his advice but before he could catch up with him a lion suddenly appeared. It was the same lion who had already lost part of his tooth. The lion was still angry and when he saw the donkey he fell on him. The lion was almost ready to kill the donkey when the frightened animal suddenly kicked with all his might and cracked open the lion's head. His brains were revealed and Obi quickly ran up and took them. "The rest of the lion is yours," he told the donkey.

Obi returned to the wizard.

"Here is the milk of a buffalo," he said to the wizard. "Here are the tears of an elephant. Here is the tooth of a lion and the tail of a monkey. Here finally are the brains of a lion."

"You have done very well," said the wizard. "Now your wife will have a child, and it will be a son."

The wizard mixed together what Obi had brought him, and together these ingredients formed a medicine which Obi gave to his wife Ngozi. Before the end of the year the childless wife had given birth to a son.

When the son grew to manhood he caught the rabbit and bought the donkey.

"You helped my father," said the son, "and now I shall help you."

Obi's son fed and protected the rabbit and the donkey for the rest of their lives.

The Present is
the Most Important Time

There was once a Chief whose mind was troubled. He was troubled because he wanted to know the answers to three questions. The first question was this: when is the most important time? The second was: who is the most important man? The third was: what is a man's most important action?

The Chief thought that if he knew the answers to these three questions, he would succeed in anything he chose to do. Moreover, he knew that if he had the answers to these three questions, he would also be respected by his people for his great wisdom.

The Chief called many people to him, many learned men, but not one of them could answer any of the three questions to his satisfaction. Then at last the Chief heard of a certain hermit who lived in the forest. This hermit was very famous for his wisdom.

The Chief therefore called for his horse, and he rode alone into the forest in search of the hermit. When he reached the hermit's home he saw a very old man digging holes and hoeing the ground. The hermit was so feeble that he could only just manage to dig and hoe and he looked very tired. The Chief jumped off his horse and greeted the old man.

"I have come to ask you three questions," said the Chief, having finished his greetings, and he asked the hermit the three questions.

The hermit listened but made no answer, all the time continuing with his work.

"You are tired," said the Chief. "Let me help you. I will dig while you rest."

The Chief dug for some time, then he repeated his questions, but instead of giving answers the hermit got up from where he was resting and said he would continue with his digging. However, the Chief would not allow that, and went on digging for the hermit.

Then suddenly the Chief saw a bearded man coming toward him, with blood flowing from wounds on his face. The Chief stopped the man with kind words, and washed his face with water from a nearby stream. Then he wrapped a cloth around the wounds. When the bearded man asked for water to drink the Chief brought it to him, after which he took the man into a hut where he could rest. The Chief also lay down to rest, for by that time night had come.

The next morning the Chief went once more to the hermit. The hermit was planting seeds in the holes that had been dug the day before.

"Oh, wise hermit," said the Chief. "I beg you to answer my three questions."

"Your questions have already been answered," replied the hermit.

"I have heard no answers," said the Chief.

"You had pity for me because of my weakness and my age," the hermit explained. "You stayed with me to help. If you had not done so and had gone on your way that bearded man would have killed you."

The Chief listened without saying a word while the hermit continued speaking.

"The most important time was when you were digging for me. It was I who was the most important man at the time and help-ing me was your most important action. When the wounded man came near us he was then the most important man and what you were doing for him was your most important action."

The Chief began to understand what the hermit's words should mean to him.

"Remember," said the hermit, "there is only one time that is important, and that time is the present. Remember, the most

important man is the man whom you are with at any moment, for you never know whether he may be the last person on earth with whom you meet. Remember, the most important action for you to do is to treat well and with justice the man you are with, because it is for that purpose alone that you were sent into this life."

Then the hermit began to sow his seeds again, and the Chief mounted his horse and rode back to his palace. Never did he forget what he had learnt from the hermit, and the fame of the Chief's goodness and wisdom spread throughout the land.

Wiser than a King

There was once a boy whose name in his own language was 'Wiser-than-a-king'.

In that part of the country there lived a powerful king. One day a monkey reported to him that there was a boy in a nearby village whose name was 'Wiser-than-a-king'.

The king was angry.

"I shall test this strangely named boy," the king decided. "Who can be wiser than a king?"

He sent the monkey and two servants to bring the boy to him. They fetched the boy and brought him before their master.

"Are you wiser than a king?" the king asked the boy.

"Sire," replied the boy, "that is not for me to say, but nevertheless, that is my name."

Then the king spoke: "I order you to cut my hair."

"Before I cut your majesty's hair, millet must be cut and prepared so that I can eat afterwards."

The king instructed his servants to cut and prepare millet. Then the boy cut the king's hair.

"Put my hair back where it was before," said the king to the boy.

"Before I put back your hair, you must put my millet back growing in the ground," replied the boy.

"How can I put the millet back?" answered the king.

"How can I put your hair back?" said the boy.

Then the king called his servants to bring corn from the granary in the palace compound. They brought the corn in baskets to where the king and the boy were facing each other.

"Take this corn," said the king to the boy. "Prepare a sweet drink from it so that I can drink it today."

The boy showed the king some seeds from the calabash plant.

"Sire," he said. "Let your servants take these seeds and plant them so that I can have calabashes in which to put the sweet corn drink today."

"How can I plant calabash seeds for the plants to grow and the calabashes to be cut, so that you can put liquid into them and all this to be done today?" the king asked.

"How can I make corn into a sweet drink for you today?" replied the boy.

The king considered these questions and answers. Finally he said to the boy, "You, who are named 'Wiser-than-a-king', bring me my horse."

The boy fetched the horse and brought it to the king.

"Now feed the horse every minute with grass," the king ordered. "If you fail, your disobedience will cause me to punish you severely."

The boy was not worried. He obtained delicious porridge made from maize and he called all the rats of the town to him. In exchange for the delicious porridge of maize, the rats agreed to bring grass every minute.

"Your horse is being fed," the boy told the king.

As they watched, they saw grass coming to the horse. The king could not see the rats underneath the grass as they carried it, but grass was coming to the horse every minute.

"I thought I was wiser than you," the surprised king admitted to the boy. "But you, you are wiser than I am, 'Wiser-than-a-king'."

The boy was then allowed to return safely to his village. He went to his house and joined his parents, where they lived happily and peacefully ever afterwards.

The Lion, the Monkey
and the Clever Bird

A young lion fell into a deep hole and could not get out. He had nothing to eat on the first day, nor on the second day, nor on the third day.

"I shall die," said the lion to himself. "I shall die of hunger."

But on the fourth day he saw a monkey high above the hole. The monkey was jumping from tree to tree.

"Monkey, monkey," cried the young lion. "Please help me."

The monkey stopped jumping and looked down at the lion in the hole.

"Certainly I shall help you," he replied. "What do you wish me to do?"

"Put your tail down into the hole," said the lion. "Then I can hold your tail and climb out of the hole. Please save me."

The monkey agreed to this plan and jumped to a branch of a tree which was directly above the hole; he put his tail down into the hole and told the lion to take hold of it. The lion caught the tail and climbed up from the hole whereupon he seized the monkey's body with his two front paws.

"Now I am going to eat you," said the lion.

"Why are you going to eat me?" cried the monkey.

"Because this is the fourth day on which I have not eaten any food," replied the lion.

"But you should not eat me," the monkey protested, "considering that it was I who saved you. You ought to thank me."

At that moment a big black bird flew down to join the lion and the monkey.

"What are you talking about so angrily?" the big black bird asked.

The monkey told the bird the whole story: how he had lowered his tail into the deep hole to save the lion, and how, instead of giving thanks, the lion had said he was going to eat him.

Then the bird said to the lion, "It is wrong for you to eat the monkey. He saved your life."

"But I am very hungry," said the lion. "If I do not eat the monkey, I shall die of starvation. This is the fourth day on which I have not eaten."

The clever bird decided to try to save the monkey's life and she thought of a plan. "Let me ask you three questions before you eat the monkey and please give me three answers."

"Very well," agreed the lion. "You may ask me three questions and I will answer you."

"My first question is this," said the bird. "Is it true that this monkey saved your life?"

"Yes, that is true," answered the lion.

"My next question," the bird continued, "is this. Is it true that this is the fourth day on which you have had nothing to eat?"

"Yes, that is true," answered the lion.

"My third question," the bird said, "is this. Did you thank the monkey for saving your life?"

"No," replied the lion, "I didn't."

The bird said, "It was wrong of you not to thank the monkey. Before you start to eat him, you should thank him for his kindness."

"Very well," the lion said, "but how shall I thank the monkey?"

The wise bird had her answer ready.

"You must thank him by holding your head down on the ground."

Then the lion took his paws from the monkey and held his head down to the ground while he was giving thanks.

"Monkey, escape. You are saved," cried the big black bird as she flew away.

"I'm saved," cried the monkey, jumping up quickly and climbing the nearest tall tree.

The ungrateful lion saw the monkey escape. However, the monkey himself had learnt a lesson: he would never help lions again.

The Rivalry
for the Lizard King's Daughters

Many years ago the King of Lizards had two beautiful daughters. Nobody except the king knew their names. The king declared that anyone who could tell him their names would be given a daughter to marry, and also a bag of money.

Naturally every man wanted to marry a daughter of the king and to have a bag of money, but no one could tell the daughters' names.

However, the monkey was particularly clever. For three days he carefully concealed himself and watched what the king's daughters were doing. On the fourth day he bought two mango fruits. They were of first-class quality and appearance. He took them and climbed one of the trees under which the girls were playing.

Eventually one of the sisters went away. Then the monkey threw down a mango. The girl under the tree called to her sister to come back and share the fruit. She called her by her name, so the clever monkey knew one of the names.

Then the monkey waited patiently until the other sister went away. Again he threw down a mango and the girl remaining under the tree also called to her sister to come back and share the fruit. She called her by name, so the monkey heard that also.

At this time there was a very important rule about speaking to the King of Lizards. Nobody was allowed to speak to him directly. If anyone wanted to speak to the king, he would speak to a palace official known as the Old Lizard who would then repeat the words to the king.

The day after the monkey had found out the names of the king's daughters, he went to the palace. All the lizards were there. The monkey told the Old Lizard that he wished to marry a daughter of the king. The Old Lizard repeated this to the king.

"What are the names of my daughters?" asked the king.

The monkey told their names to the Old Lizard and the Old Lizard repeated them to the king.

"It is to you that I will give both my daughters and the two bags of money," the king announced to the Old Lizard. "They are yours, Old Lizard, because you have spoken their names to me."

The monkey was very angry. He waited until night time. In the darkness he stole a large cock which belonged to the king. He killed the cock and ate it; then he went to the house of the Old Lizard. He threw the bones and the feathers of the cock into the Old Lizard's house.

"But I am not yet finished," said the monkey to himself.

Next he heated some palm-tree juice and took it to the Old Lizard.

"Drink this sweet-tasting juice," persuaded the monkey. The Old Lizard foolishly drank it and burnt his throat.

The monkey then took some more heated palm-tree juice to the Old Lizard's servant.

"Drink this sweet-tasting juice," said the monkey, and the unsuspecting servant drank it and burnt his throat also.

The next morning it was reported to the king that one of his best cocks was missing. Everyone was called to the palace.

"Where is my cock?" the king demanded.

"The Old Lizard stole it," cried the monkey. "The bones and feathers are in his house."

"Is it you who has stolen my cock?" the king asked the Old Lizard.

But the Old Lizard's throat had been so badly burnt by the hot palm-tree juice that he could not speak; he could only nod his head up and down.

"Was it the Old Lizard who stole my cock?" the king asked the Old Lizard's servant.

But the Old Lizard's servant had burnt his throat so badly by drinking the hot palm-tree juice that he, too, was unable to speak. He could only nod his head up and down.

Then the king spoke to all those who were gathered together at the palace: "Even though the Old Lizard told me the names of my daughters, it appears that he has stolen my cock. Therefore I shall give to the Old Lizard neither my daughters nor the two bags of money."

So neither the Old Lizard nor the monkey married a daughter of the king nor received a bag of money.

The Superiority of a Man
Twenty-five Years Old

Once upon a time a handsome lion and a striped hyena were close friends. One day the lion said to the hyena, "Of all living creatures, which do you dread the most?"

"It is the wild bull I fear," replied the hyena. "He breaks branches of trees, tramples on ant hills and roars with such a frightening voice that all his enemies tremble."

The hyena asked the lion which of all living creatures *he* feared the most.

"More than all and certainly more than a wild bull," replied the lion, "I fear a man who is twenty-five years old."

"What nonsense," exclaimed the hyena. "I will readily defeat twenty-five men each aged twenty-five if you will overcome even one wild bull."

"We shall meet this evening," said the lion, "and we shall see."

That evening the hyena came to meet the lion whom he found busy washing his handsome mane. The two friends greeted each other.

"I hope you have not forgotten our agreement," said the hyena. "As for me, I am a creature of my words. They are as strong to me as my own bones."

"Our agreement is not forgotten," the lion replied. "Choose a wild bull and I will overcome him."

The lion and the hyena hid themselves by a path. Soon several bush cows appeared and near them a wild bull breaking branches off trees, trampling on ant hills and roaring very loudly. The hyena pointed to the bull and he trembled as he said to the lion, "Try to defeat *that* one."

The lion sprang at the wild bull. There was a short fight. The lion easily won: he and the hyena ate the defeated bull for dinner.

The next evening the lion and the hyena went to the same path and hid themselves. Soon a man twenty-five years old appeared. He had a big stick in one hand and some food in a bowl in the other.

"Try to defeat *that* one," said the lion.

The hyena rushed at the man but the man paid very little attention and walked calmly on, saying, "Hyena, be more careful. You are raising dust and it is settling on my food."

The hyena rushed at the man again and again; the man paid little attention, only reproving him for raising so much dust. The lion laughed at the hyena.

When the hyena rushed at the man for a third time, the man became impatient. He hit the hyena with his stick so hard on the head that the top of the stick broke off and hit the lion in the eye.

"Hyena, what did I tell you?" cried the lion as he ran away.

After the hyena recovered from the blow he had received on his head he joined the lion, who was still rubbing his eye.

The two friends decided that in future they would not attack men and certainly never a man twenty-five years old.

The Magic Cooking Pot

There was an old woman who sold the best palm-oil soup in the market. Nobody knew the old woman's name nor where she lived. Nobody knew how she made such excellent soup nor why the soup was always so hot.

"This is a mystery," the people at the market would say to each other, but continued to buy the soup.

Every morning the old woman came into the market-place by the village carrying a big black pot of hot palm-oil soup on her head. Then she sat under a tall mango tree and soon all her soup was sold, for it was so good.

There was a boy in the village called Kalari. He had often enjoyed the old woman's soup and he wanted to know how it was made. He wanted to know where the old woman lived.

Small boys are often curious and one evening when the market closed, Kalari followed the old woman. He followed her through the village and beside the river. Keeping himself out of sight, he followed her along a path that went up the side of a hill. Kalari began to be afraid. Nevertheless, he forced himself to continue and followed the old woman until she came to a small round hut with mud bricks for the walls and a grass thatch roof.

Outside the hut stood a very large cooking pot.

"It is the biggest pot," thought Kalari, "that I have ever seen."

The old woman went inside the hut. Kalari was so curious that he went quietly to the pot and looked inside. It was empty.

Hearing the old woman coming out of the hut, he hid himself behind some thorn bushes. He watched the old woman come out of the hut. She went to the very large cooking pot and, raising her arms above her head, she sang this song:

"Magic pot, magic pot,
Make hot soup for me.
Make hot soup for me.
Make soup of palm-oil.
Make soup of palm-oil.
Make soup with chicken.
Make soup, this soup, for me to sell.
For people to buy.
Magic pot, magic pot."

From where Kalari was hidden he could soon hear the soup boiling and bubbling, and he saw steam coming from the pot. The smell of the soup was so good that it made Kalari feel hungry. When the old woman went back into her hut, he came softly from behind the thorn bushes.

Kalari looked under the pot. There was no fire beneath it. He looked into the pot: it was full of hot palm-oil soup with chicken.

"I must taste this," said Kalari to himself, putting his hand into the pot to select a piece of chicken.

But suddenly the old woman came out of her hut. She saw Kalari and what he was doing.

"Oh! Oh! Oh!" cried the old woman. "Oh! Oh! Oh!"

Kalari was filled with fear. He turned and ran down the hillside path as fast as he could. Behind him he could hear the old woman. She was screaming and wailing, shouting and crying.

Kalari ran and ran until he reached the bottom of the hill. He ran beside the river. He ran until he passed the market and reached the village. He ran to the house of his family. He told his parents and the people of the village what had happened. He pointed to the hill. As the people looked at the hill they could see steam rising from it.

"The magic pot," everyone said to everyone else.

From that day until this the old woman with her pot of chicken and palm-oil soup has never returned to the market. No one has ever gone up the hill to search for her, least of all Kalari. When clouds gather near the top of the hill the village people say to each other, "Look, there is the steam from the magic cooking pot."

The Tortoise is not as clever as he sometimes thinks

A chief called a meeting of all the people and animals whom he ruled. All the chief's councillors were also present. He called them together in order to give them laws, one of which was that no one should eat yam for six months.

"Must we ourselves also obey these laws?" the councillors asked the chief.

The chief told them that they also must obey the laws.

One of the councillors was the tortoise. He stood up and asked if the chief, himself, were excluded.

"No," the chief replied, "why should I be excluded from my own laws?"

"Your honour," continued the tortoise, "what is the punishment for you if you break one of these laws?"

"If I happened to break one of my own laws," said the chief, "I should lose my position as your chief."

The meeting came to an end and the councillors went off to their own households. So did all the people and the animals who had attended. The chief mounted his horse and went to his own house.

Some days later several of the councillors gathered together secretly to discuss how they might make the chief disobey one of his own laws.

"He would then lose his position and one of us would be chief," they said.

"I know a way to catch the chief breaking his laws," said the tortoise.

The other councillors asked what the tortoise's plan was, but he said he must keep this a secret. Then the lion announced the time and place of the next council meeting.

On that day, the tortoise took a very fresh, fat yam and cooked it. When it was ready, he took the yam and went to a certain shady, isolated place. This place was by the path which the chief would be taking when he came to the meeting. The tortoise left the yam in a bowl by the path. Then he hid himself under some leaves and waited.

Soon the chief came along the road. He was riding his horse slowly and he was hungry. When he saw the bowl he stopped the horse, dismounted and saw the well-cooked, sweet-smelling yam. The chief looked in all directions but he could see no one. He went to the bowl and ate a piece of the yam.

"Chief, have you eaten yam?" the tortoise shouted from where he was hidden under the leaves.

The chief was startled. He looked again in all directions. Again he saw no one. He returned to the bowl and took another piece of yam.

The tortoise shouted again, "Chief, have you eaten yam?"

The chief again looked for someone and then he observed the cunning tortoise under the leaves. The chief apologized, asking pardon of the tortoise and requesting him not to report the matter. But the tortoise refused and paid no attention to the words of the chief.

"We shall have to go to the meeting anyway," said the chief. So he mounted his horse and the tortoise followed.

They reached the meeting place where the councillors were all waiting. As usual, the chief was given the seat of honour, but when he sat down the tortoise shouted, "Chief, who has eaten yam?"

At once the chief gave up his seat of honour and then the tortoise stopped shouting. The chief sat on a small piece of wood beside the councillors.

Food and drink were brought. When the chief was taking his own share, the tortoise immediately shouted again, "Chief, who has eaten yam?"

Silently, the chief gave what he had to the tortoise and again the tortoise stopped shouting. But the chief had become angry and as soon as the meeting was over, he mounted his horse, saying:

"Remember, councillors, that I am more powerful still than any of you."

Then he suddenly seized the tortoise and rode away with him.

"Help! Help!" the tortoise cried, but neither the lion nor any of the other councillors came to his rescue.

After riding for some time, while the tortoise complained incessantly, they reached a very rocky place. The rocks there were hard and sharp.

"Now you will be punished," cried the chief and he flung the tortoise against the rocks.

From that day until this, the tortoise has always moved awkwardly as if he still feels his body full of pain.

The Greedy Hare

A hare was invited to go and eat at the house of his wife's family. Wanting a companion on the way, he arranged for one of the lambs of a neighbouring sheep to go with him. They started on their journey.

Although the hare was glad of a companion he did not want to share the meal that was awaiting him. So the hare played a trick. He and the lamb came to two stones lying beside the path. The hare told the lamb to hide the stones and to be sure to remember where they were hidden.

"We shall soon be needing the stones," said the hare.

As soon as the hare finished speaking he started to run very fast. The lamb followed with difficulty. They passed a gourd and the broken pieces of an old pot. The hare called to the lamb to hide these articles and to be sure to remember where.

"We shall soon be needing them," cried the hare.

At last they reached the house of the hare's wife's family. After many greetings and good wishes, palm kernels were brought to be eaten. At once, the hare told the lamb to fetch the hidden stones. The lamb went as fast as he could, but that was not very fast because he was so tired after his long run with the hare. When the lamb returned, the hare had eaten three-quarters of the palm kernels. The hare said to the lamb, "To be fair, I shall give you half of what remains."

Then the hare's wife's family brought loaves of bread for the hare and the lamb to eat. Immediately the hare told the lamb to fetch the gourd and the broken pieces of the old pot. By the time the lamb returned, only one small loaf of bread remained.

"To be fair," said the hare, "I shall give you half of the loaf that remains."

The lamb was very hungry by the time he and the hare started on the return journey, while the hare's stomach was full. The lamb decided that he would not accompany the hare on journeys again.

The next time the hare was going to visit the house of his wife's family, he asked a friend of his, a bird, to accompany him. The bird had beautiful feathers, with two long tail feathers, and he was of the royal family of birds.

On their way they saw two stones. The hare told the bird to hide the stones.

"We shall soon be needing the stones," he said. But the bird had a bag with him and he put the stones into the bag instead.

Then the hare started to run very fast. But the bird flew above the hare, travelling even faster than the hare.

They reached a gourd and the broken pieces of another old pot. The hare called to the bird to hide these articles.

"We shall soon be needing them," he said.

The bird put them inside his bag, then flew on, closely following the hare.

When the hare and the bird reached the hare's wife's family's house, the bird hung the bag outside the door. After the usual greetings and salutations palm kernels were brought.

"Fetch the stones," the hare ordered the bird.

The bird went out to his bag and quickly brought the stones to the hare, then ate half the palm kernels. Loaves of bread were brought.

"Fetch the gourd and the broken pieces of the old pot," ordered the hare.

The bird went out to his bag and quickly brought these articles to the hare, then ate half the loaves. Next the hare's wife's family brought some beans.

"I shall take these to my wife," said the hare, who did not wish to share them with the bird. He poured them into a bag of his own.

"I shall leave you now," said the bird, pretending to fly away, but he returned very quietly and hid in the hare's bag.

The hare thanked his wife's family, took up his bag, and started on the return journey.

"At least I shall have all the beans for myself," he thought, and when he reached his home he entered very carefully so that his wife would not see the bag. But when he opened the bag he could not see a single bean, not even a grain. There was only the bird, who quickly flew out of the bag laughing at the hare and crying: "I have much enjoyed your company, you greedy hare. I hope you have enjoyed mine."

The Tortoise and his Broken Shell

There was a famine in a certain town. Every creature in that town was hungry except a dog who knew of a tree in the nearby forest which supplied him with food. No one but the dog knew where he obtained his food.

Now there lived in the town a tortoise and his wife. They were so hungry they would watch the dog to see what he threw away and then they would eat the scraps. Finally the tortoise and his wife spoke to the dog: "Neighbour dog, we can no longer endure our sufferings of hunger. Tell us where you obtain your food."

After they had begged the dog many times to tell them, he at last revealed his secret, on the strict promise that they would tell no one. They promised. The dog showed them the tree in the forest on which the food grew and allowed them to eat there.

135

But the tortoise and his wife abused their good fortune. They went to the tree when they knew the dog was not there. They ate until they could hardly move and when they did go away, they took with them an enormous basket filled with food.

One day when the dog went to the tree to have his breakfast he noticed that a great portion of the food was gone. The dog hid himself and watched to see who might come. As he watched he saw the tortoise and his wife approaching.

The tortoise and his wife were pushing their enormous basket. The dog waited until they began to pick the food from the tree. Then he jumped out at them, barking furiously.

"Now I will kill you," shouted the dog to the trembling tortoise.

The tortoise begged for mercy, then turned and ran until he found a swamp in which to hide. But the dog chased him and taking a big stick tried to catch the tortoise. Every time the tortoise was struck with the stick he sang in pretended joy and every time the dog missed him he cried as if in pain. Then a wise man came to watch the dog and explained the tortoise's trick. The dog quickly managed to catch hold of the tortoise after that, dragged him out of the swamp and threw him so hard against the side of a very hard tree trunk that his shell was cracked and broken.

The dog left, thinking the tortoise would die. But tortoises are strong little creatures and the tortoise began to recover. A passing traveller knocked his foot against the tortoise thinking it was a stone. Always cunning, the tortoise cried out, "Look what you have done. You have broken my shell."

"My job," said the traveller, "is to repair broken articles."

"If that is your job," said the tortoise, "you should be able to repair my shell."

The traveller produced his tools from the bag he was carrying. He put together the many pieces of broken tortoise-shell. Even today we can see that the shell of a tortoise is of many pieces which have been put together.

The Cricket and the Toad

There were once two friends, a cricket and a toad. During the season of the rains they worked together farming. Every day they left their village and walked along the path until they reached the clearing in the bush where they did their farming. They worked hard, turning the ground and preparing it for planting. Every day they took beans and oil to cook and eat when they became tired and hungry.

One day the cricket and the toad found that their supplies of oil were finished and so they could only cook beans. That day they had worked harder than ever before and so they were very tired and very hungry.

"We must rest and eat our beans," said the toad. "I am sorry that we have no oil today."

"Make a fire," replied the cricket. "Put a pot of beans on the fire and I shall make oil."

The toad made the fire, put the pot of beans on it, and, after instructing the toad what to do, the cricket jumped into the pot. Then the toad did what he had been told and he sang a song:

> "Make oil, make oil,
> So we may use oil,
> While eating our cooked beans."

The toad repeated the song several times and the cricket made oil from his body. Then the cricket jumped out and he and the toad started eating their meal. Every day the cricket jumped into the pot, making oil for the beans while the toad sang the cricket's song. Finally, the toad said to the cricket, "Tomorrow I shall make the oil for our beans."

The next day the two friends went to their farms and they worked as usual. When they were ready to eat, the cricket prepared a large fire and placed a cooking pot almost full of beans on top of the flames. The toad jumped in and the cricket began to sing the song:

> "Make oil, make oil,
> So we may use oil,
> While eating our cooked beans."

The cricket repeated the song many times, but there was no oil from the toad. Then the fire grew hotter and the toad started to sing:

> "Oh, cricket, save me.
> For my life's sake, save me.
> I am dying."

Quickly the cricket began to put out the large fire, but before it was quenched and the toad could be rescued, he had swollen almost to the point of bursting. When the flames had disappeared the toad jumped out, leaving all the beans so burnt that they could not be eaten. He and the cricket had nothing to eat that day. The toad's body was not only swollen, but also his back was scratched and hard.

Since that time toads are swollen and almost on the point of bursting when they are angry. It is the laughing of the cricket, making jokes at the expense of his friend the toad, which some people say is the sound one hears from the cricket's hole by night.

The Pig's search for a Grinding Stone

Here is a story of the tortoise and the pig, two travelling traders. They bought, they journeyed to other markets and they sold what they had bought. But although their activities were the same, they were not equally successful. The pig became rich, while the tortoise grew poor.

Finally the tortoise planned to run away in order to escape from the men to whom he owed money. But the tortoise's wife had a better idea and she went to see the pig. She told him all about her husband's troubles.

"Please help us," begged the tortoise's wife.

The pig made enquiries and he discovered that what the tortoise's wife had told him was true. So he lent the tortoise a large sum of money. That night the tortoise and his wife celebrated. The next day they went to the pig to thank him and it was agreed that the money should be returned after twelve months had passed.

The tortoise and his wife bought much food and clothing. They decided that instead of risking failure in their trading they would farm.

"The money from the sale of the crop on the farm," said the tortoise's wife, "will be enough to repay the pig."

But the tortoise was lazy. For months he did nothing. Every day his wife asked when he would start farming and every day the tortoise replied that he would start at some future date. Every day, however, the tortoise would pass the time sitting and talking with his friends and buying coloured cloths and many sweet things to eat and drink.

The end of the twelve months came and there was no farm. Nearly all the borrowed money was gone. The pig sent a servant to ask the tortoise to bring the money, but the tortoise sent back a message saying he was too ill to come. Shortly afterwards the tortoise was cutting firewood when the pig unexpectedly arrived. The pig said he was surprised that the tortoise's recovery from illness had been so rapid. The tortoise replied that the servant must have given the wrong message. He was too busy, not too ill, to come.

"Very well," said the pig. "But it is now time for you to repay me my money."

"I have all but one fraction of the money at the moment," the tortoise lied. "You will be repaid when I have the full amount."

"I would be pleased to have all but that fraction now," said the pig.

"Wait until tomorrow," the tortoise insisted. "I have some maize which I shall sell in the market."

The pig agreed and returned to his house, while the tortoise and his wife planned how they might solve their difficulties.

The next day the pig reappeared. He was angry that the tortoise had not come to him already with the money. The tortoise

quickly lay on his back with a small stone on his chest so that he looked like a grinding stone.

When the pig entered the tortoise's house he saw only the tortoise's wife. She said that her husband had gone out and she did not know when he might be back.

With a cry of anger, the pig seized what he thought was a grinding stone and threw it away into the forest as far as it would go. He did not bother to see where it landed. He did not know he had thrown away the tortoise.

Immediately the tortoise's wife began to shout and cry.

"This pig has thrown away my grinding stone," she complained in a loud voice. A crowd of villagers gathered. The tortoise then joined the crowd, pretending that he had just returned from a short walk.

"That grinding stone was a very special one," said the tortoise to the pig. "It cost me the amount of money you lent to me. Until you find my grinding stone I cannot repay the money you lent me."

The pig hurried off to the forest but of course he could not find what he was looking for. He looked everywhere. He dug in the ground with his snout. He has been breaking ground and searching ever since.

The Poor Man who became King

In a country of many hills there was a city called the Great City. A poor man lived there whose name was Karang. He had no wife and very little to eat.

Poor Karang begged for his food. People gave him the food they themselves did not want. Karang was a man with a kind, friendly and polite manner. Because of this the people of the city and also the animals liked him.

The king of the Great City owned a very fat cow. He fed the cow so well that it continued to grow fatter and fatter. Karang saw the cow and an idea came to him that would free him from his poverty and begging.

He thought to himself, "I shall ask the king to let me eat that fat cow. In exchange the king can take me as a slave. That will be the end of my difficulties."

Karang went to the palace of the king. The king was sitting outside. After Karang had greeted him, he told the king his plan. In exchange for eating the king's fat cow Karang said he would become one of the king's slaves.

"I agree with this suggestion," said the king, and he gave orders that the fat cow should be prepared for Karang to eat. "You may eat this cow for three days," the king said, "and at the end of the third day you will become my own property."

The cow was cooked and on the first day Karang began to eat. He was eating near a tall tree and in the tree was a bird's nest in which were some young birds. The little birds were crying for something to eat. Karang gave them some of his own food.

When the mother bird returned to her nest, the young birds refused the meat she had brought them.

"Why do you refuse to eat?" she asked and they replied, "Our stomachs are full. The man who is eating the cow beneath this tree has already given us meat."

The next day Karang was still eating near the tall tree and again he heard the little birds crying for something to eat. Again he gave them some of his own food.

When the mother bird returned to the nest, the young birds again did not wish to eat what she had brought them.

"Has this man fed you again?" she asked, and the young birds replied that he had.

On the third day, the mother bird decided to wait to see the man who had been so kind to her young birds. The young birds cried for food and the man came bringing meat.

"Why have you so much to eat," the bird asked, "that every day you are able to feed my young birds?"

"The king gave me his fat cow so that I could eat it and then become his slave," Karang answered.

"When will you become a slave?" asked the bird.

"Today," the man answered.

Then the bird said, "When you are taken in front of the king of the Great City, you should do the following."

"What shall I do?" asked Karang.

"Ask the king to let you say your last words of freedom," the bird continued. "When you are given this chance, you must say, 'Is this the end of my life as a free man?' Then, I shall help you."

Karang returned to what remained of his food from the fat cow and continued to eat until it was time for him to go to the king's palace. The bird flew to a place where she could watch what was happening.

When Karang was brought to him to be put in chains of bondage, the king was present with all his people.

Karang said, "Please allow me to say my last words of freedom."

The king and his people said, "Say your last words."

Karang lifted up his head and cried, "Is this the end of my life as a free man?"

Then a great voice from the sky, which in fact was the bird, came like thunder.

"If anyone enslaves you, Karang, there will be no rain on this country for three years. The crops will die. There will be hunger and starvation."

The great voice repeated the threat many times.

The people were filled with fear. The king was filled with fear also. He declared, "Is it the poor who are the most powerful? Who am I to be ruling Karang?"

The king gave his title to Karang who became king. The former king was content to serve him. Believing that the sky would answer Karang, the people accepted him as their new king of the Great City.

In his heart Karang was forever grateful to the bird who saved him from slavery and made him a king.

Another Cause of Enmity between the Cat and the Rat

L ong ago before cats and rats were enemies, a cat and a rat were on a journey together. They reached the side of a very wide river.

"How shall we cross?" asked the cat.

"We need a boat," the rat replied.

"There is no boat here," said the cat.

"In that case," the rat answered, "we shall have to find something else which can be used as a boat."

The rat led the way to a nearby yam farm and being an experienced thief, he did not hesitate about going to a ridge and pulling out one of the biggest yams. The rat asked the cat to help and the cat did so.

As they were leaving the farm with the yam, the owner of the farm came upon them. The cat ran up a tree, but the rat ran along the ground and only just managed to escape being caught.

After the farmer had gone, the rat returned and blamed the cat for not carrying him up the tree.

"Let us not quarrel," said the cat. "Let us make haste to cross the river."

Then the rat gnawed at the yam until he had made it into the shape of a boat. The two animals launched their yam boat, put in their loads, climbed in themselves, and started to cross the river.

Now the river was very wide and before they had crossed half way the friends had finished the food they had brought and were hungry.

"Let us sleep," said the rat. "We must try to forget our hunger."

The cat and rat went to sleep, but soon the rat woke again because of his great hunger. He began to gnaw at the yam boat. After some time the sound of gnawing woke the cat.

"What have you been doing while I was sleeping?" the cat asked. "I heard a peculiar noise."

"I've been doing nothing except sleeping," the rat answered. "You must have heard me snoring."

The journey across the river continued. The cat had nothing to eat, but every time he slept the rat would eat more of the boat. At last when they were nearing the other side of the river the rat gnawed a hole in the bottom of the boat and water started to pour in.

"Ah," cried the cat as he and the rat leapt ashore, "I see how you have been cheating me and endangering my life."

At once the cat seized the rat in his paws and began to eat him. The taste of the rat was so sweet that he ate him all up. Thus all cats soon began to enjoy eating rats, and from that day they became enemies.

The Singing Bird
and the Dancing Farmer

Not so very long ago there lived a farmer whose name was Simon. He was a sensible, hard-working man. Every year at planting-time he cleared his land. He planted yams, maize and cassava, but mainly yams. Thus Simon would see that his family did not go hungry; he and his wife and his many children would always have enough to eat.

Now it was time for preparing the farm again.

"I shall go to the farm today," he told his wife, "and take a cutlass to start clearing the land."

Simon left the village and went along a narrow path to the place where he would make his farm.

"Good," he said to himself. "Here is suitable family land. Here I will grow our next year's food supply, but before planting I must clear away the underbrush and bushes."

Simon picked up his cutlass, but he had hardly set to work when he heard the loud, shrill sound of a bird singing. The song was very beautiful, and Simon could not resist the rhythm; flinging down his cutlass he began to dance. At last, when he was quite exhausted, the bird stopped singing. But as soon as Simon picked up his cutlass the song began again and Simon found himself compelled to drop the cutlass and dance. Each time he tried to work the bird started singing and Simon was compelled to dance again and again.

After seven attempts to work Simon became desperate.

"This wicked bird," he cried. "How can I clear the farm and do my planting?"

Simon ran back to the village. He went to his elderly uncle, a much respected man, and told him the story.

"You are talking nonsense," said the uncle. But Simon repeated so earnestly how the singing bird was interfering with his work that the uncle suspected there might be some truth in his story.

"Very well," he said to his nephew, Simon. "We shall go back to the farm and I shall see if what you say is true."

Simon and his uncle returned to the farm. Simon picked up his cutlass and started clearing. Immediately the bird began to sing high up in a mahogany tree. Once again Simon had to abandon his work and dance.

"Stop, stop," cried the uncle. "Give me your cutlass."

He gave his uncle the cutlass. The uncle began clearing the bushes and the underbrush. At once, the bird began to sing again. The uncle found himself caught by the song. Throwing down the cutlass he started to dance and could only rest when the singing stopped.

"This is very serious," said the uncle. "We must go back to the village and inform the Chief."

They hurried back along the path, past other farms already cleared and planted. When they reached the village they went to the Chief's big house. They were taken to the veranda where he was sitting on a carved and decorated wooden chair.

"Oh, Chief," said Simon, bowing politely, "I have a terrible thing to report."

"What terrible thing?" asked the chief.

"My family and I," replied Simon, "will soon starve to death. A singing bird is preventing me from preparing my farm."

"What foolish talk is this?" the Chief exclaimed in an angry voice. But after Simon had told his story the Chief was angrier than ever. "You are bothering me with something I cannot believe."

Then Simon's uncle, who was much respected for his age and wisdom, asked permission to speak.

"What Simon says is true," he said, and explained how he himself had tried to work and how the singing bird had made him dance instead. "If you go to that farm," the uncle concluded, "you too will dance."

For several minutes the Chief sat silently but in deep thought. Suddenly he stood up.

"There is a mystery here," he said. "We will go to that farm."

So the Chief, the Chief's chair carrier carrying the carved and decorated chair, Simon's uncle and Simon himself all went out of the village and along the path to Simon's farm. The bird was still sitting high up in the mahogany tree.

The Chief sat down on his chair. "Start working," he ordered Simon. Simon took up his cutlass and had hardly set to work when the bird began to sing. Throwing down the cutlass Simon began to dance and dance until he was exhausted.

Next the Chief ordered Simon's uncle to start work. The uncle took up his cutlass and had hardly set to work before the bird began to sing. Throwing down the cutlass the uncle began to dance.

"I am a Chief," the Chief cried. "Birds cannot rule me." Jumping up from his chair he seized the cutlass and began clearing the bushes. Immediately the bird began to sing. For several seconds the Chief resisted and then he threw down the cutlass and danced until the bird stopped singing.

"We must return to the village at once," ordered the Chief. Then he, his carrier with the chair, Simon's uncle and Simon quickly returned to the village and to the Chief's house.

"Call together all the people of the village," he ordered. When they were assembled he told every man to fetch his cutlass, then to follow him back to Simon's farm. The men of the village did so, and when they arrived the Chief told them to start clearing. As soon as they picked up their cutlasses and began to work, the bird started to sing. Throwing down his cutlass every one of them danced.

In the village that night the Chief and his people discussed the problem. There was no other land for Simon and if he and his family were to have food they would have to start planting without further delay.

"Call all hunters," the Chief cried. When they came he spoke very seriously to them. "Hunting is your job. We shall see how well you hunt."

The hunters were instructed to go to Simon's farm and to catch the singing bird. On arrival at the farm they aimed their guns and fired at the bird; the bird flew rapidly from tree to tree and escaped the bullets. They shot their arrows and threw their spears at the bird. Again the bird flew rapidly from tree to tree and escaped harm.

"Shall we, our whole village, never conquer this singing bird?" cried Simon, for he had accompanied the hunters.

Then one young hunter noticed that the bird was perched on a low bough of the tree. Some boys from the village began to throw stones. The bird started to fly to a higher bough but the young hunter, who had crept very close, jumped up and caught the bird by the feet.

"I've caught it, I've caught it," announced the young hunter.

"I'm singing, I'm singing," the bird replied, fluttering its wings. But the magic had left the bird's voice. It was taken to the Chief's house.

"We will keep it in a cage," declared the Chief.

From then on the bird could sing every day, and the people would dance, but only when they pleased. No one was prevented from doing his work, and Simon returned to his farm.

He cleared it, planted his yams, his maize and his cassava, and food for his family was assured for the coming year.